DETROIT STUDIES IN MUSIC BIBLIOGRAPHY
General Editor
BRUNO NETTL
University of Illinois at Urbana-Champaign

lute, vihuela

guitar to 1800: a bibliography david b. lyons

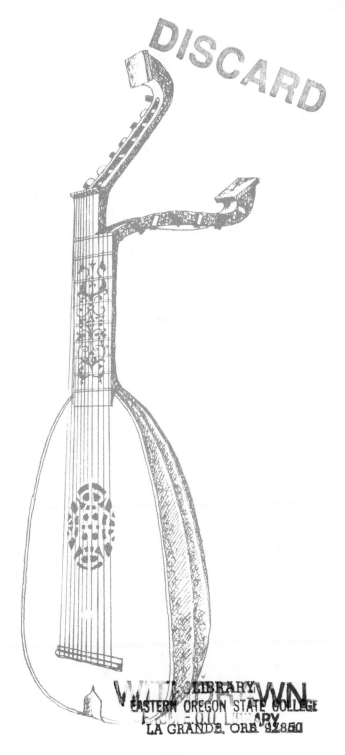

ETROIT   1978

Published by
Information Coordinators, Inc.
1435-37 Randolph Street, Detroit, Michigan 48226

Book designed by Vincent Kibildis
Illustration of theorbo, a 17th-century lute, by Lena Lyons

To
Lena, My Family
and to Frank Salazar

CONTENTS

INTRODUCTION

THE COMPLETION of Volume 8 of Die *Musik in Geschichte und Gegenwart* in 1960 provided the first complete listing of both printed and manuscript sources of lute music as well as a bibliography. Although now out of date, it still provides access to a basic bibliographic list. The next major step towards bibliographic control of the periodical literature about the lute was Ernst Pohlmann's *Laute, Theorbe, Chitarrone* (1968), which has since been revised twice, mainly in Chapter 1 which concerns the primary music sources and Chapter 7 which deals with the description of historical instruments. Its organization is a listing (Chapter 5) by author of periodical literature cross-indexed from Chapter 1—the main composer/ source index.

The period from 1500-1800 was chosen because it represents actual historical boundries. This period is the one in which the primary form of notation is tablature and the strings are in pairs or courses. After 1800 the lute disappeared as a solo instrument and reappeared as a single-string folk instrument using staff notation and could still be found in Germany and Sweden prior to the Second World War. The guitar evolved into a single-string instrument somewhat before 1800 and became basically what we know as the classic guitar of today. The orpharion, vihuela, bandora, theorbo and cittern had their beginning and end during this period and their appearance today is the result of a revived interest in early music, authentic instruments and performance.

The present work is intended to offer a more comprehensive listing of both periodical and monographic literature concerning not only the lute but also the guitar, vihuela, theorbo and related instruments (i.e. orpharion, bandora, mandolin and so forth). It also offers a listing of music editions which have either parallel tablature or a separate tablature fascicle (with a few exceptions of historic importance). No guitar transcriptions (generally) have been included because the rapidly growing body of works with the original tablature included would make such a list otherwise too cumbersome. An additional aspect of the present work is the list of reviews, not to be found elsewhere.

This bibliography is organized into twenty-eight subject divisions, the numerical entries of which are numbered consecutively from 1 to 1735. The subject divisions are organized in several ways, the method being appropriate to each specific division. For example, the first three subject divisions are arranged alphabetically by author surname. The largest section composer/performer—is arranged by composer surname, the accompanying literature by author surname. The category lute history has two subdivisions, one general, the other by country. The manuscript section is divided by country, city-library, and shelf-list number. The list of editions is by composer surname with the exception of several collective publications which are entered under the editor's surname. The section on musical form is alphabetically arranged by form (i.e. aria, dance, song, and so forth), the accompanying literature arranged by author surname. The last section requiring explanation is the review section which has only short-title entries (all works reviewed except recordings can be found as complete entries under the appropriate section) arranged by composer (for musical works) by artist (for recordings) and title (for all monographs).

To provide as comprehensive a coverage as possible, there is at the end of each division or subdivision a *See Also* section which provides other pertinent cross-references.

ABBREVIATIONS

AfMf	Archiv für Musikforschung
AfMw	Archiv für Musikwissenschaft
AMl	Acta Musicologica
AMu	Analecta Musicologica
AmZ	Allgemeine musikalische Zeitung
AnM	Anuario Musical
AnnMl	Annales Musicologiques
BAMS	Bulletin of the American Musicological Association
BJ	Bach Jahrbuch
CdM	Caecilia en de Muziek
CNRS	Centre Nationale de la Recherche Scientifique
DTÖ	Denkmäler der Tonkunst in Österreich
ed.	editor, edition, edited by
ELS	English Lutenist-Songwriters series
EM	Early Music
esp.	especially
facs.	facsimile
Festschrift ADLER	Studien zur Musikgeschichte. Festschrift für Guido Adler zum 75. Geburtstag. Wien: Universal, 1930
Festschrift APEL	"To Willi Apel on His Seventieth Birthday." (Musica Disciplina 17, 1963, pp. 7-237)
Festschrift BESSELER	Festschrift Heinrich Besseler zum sechzigsten Geburtstag. Leipzig: VEB Deutscher Verlag für Musik, 1961

Abbreviations

Festschrift CHYBINSKI	Ksiega pamiatkowa ku czci profesora Dr. Adolfa Chybinskiego ofiarowana przez uczniow i przyjaciol z okazji piecdziesiantej rocznicy urodzin i dwadziestej piatei racznicy jego pracy naukowej (1880-1905-1930)
Festschrift FEDOROV	Mélanges offerts à Vladimir Fedorov à l'occasion de son soixantee cinqieme anniversaire 5 Août, 1966. Fontis Artis Musicae 13, 1966, 1-152. Kassel: Barenreiter, 1966
Festschrift FELLERER	Festschrift Karl Gustav Fellerer zum sechzigsten Geburtstag am 7. Juli 1962 uberreicht von Freunden und Schulern. Regensburg: Bosse, 1962
Festschrift GEIRINGER	Studies in 18th Century Music. To Dr. Geiringer. N.Y. and OUP, 1970
Festschrift KOCZIRZ	Festschrift Adolph Koczirz zum 60. Geburtstag. Wien: Strache, [1930]
Festschrift KRETZSCHMAR	Festschrift Hermann Kretzschmar zum siebzigsten Geburtstag uberreicht von Kollegen, Schulern und Freunden. Leipzig: Peters, 1918
Festschrift KROYER	Festschrift Theodore Kroyer zum sechzigsten Geburtstag an 9 September, 1933 uberreicht von Freunden und Schulern. Regenburg: Bosse, 1933
Festschrift LA LAURENCIE	Mélanges de musicologie offerts à M. Lionel de la Laurencie. Paris: Droz, 1933
Festschrift LENAERTS	Renaissance-muziek 1400-1600 donum natum licium Rene Bernard Lenaerts. Leuven: Katholieke University, 1969
Festschrift MASSON	Mélanges d'histoire et d'esthétique musicales offerts à P-M Masson. Paris: Masse, [1955]
Festschrift NEUSS	Wilhelm Neuss zum 80. Geburtstag . . . 24 Juli, 1960. Munster Westfalen: Aschendorffsche Verlagsbuchhandlung, 1960
Festschrift PLAMENAC	Essays in Music in Honor of Dragan Plamenac on His 70th Birthday. Pittsburg: University of Pittsburg, 1969
Festschrift REIMANN	Gesammelte Studien; Hugo Reimann zum sechzigsten Geburtstag uberreicht von Freunden und Schulern. Leipzig: Hesse, 1909

Abbreviations

Festschrift WIORA	Historische und systematische Musikwissenschaft; ausgewählte Aufsätze von Walter Wiora. Tutzing: Schneider, 1972
GR	Guitar Review
Grove	Grove, Dictionary of Music and Musicians, 5th edition, 1970
GSJ	Galpin Society Journal
HdN	Wolf, J. Handbuch der Notationskunde
IFr	Il Fronimo
JAMS	Journal of the American Musicological Society
JLSA	Journal of the Lute Society of America
KONGRESS 1903	Atti del Congresso Internazionale di Scienze Storiche, 1903 (1905)
KONGRESS 1909	Kongress Bericht der Internationalen Musikgesellschaft, Wein 1909
KONGRESS 1911	Report of the Fourth Congress on the International Musical Society, London 1911. London: Novello, 1912
KONGRESS 1924	Kongress Bericht der Internationalen Musikgesellschaft, Basel, 1924. Leipzig, 1925
KONGRESS 1930	Report of the International Society for Musical Research. First Congress Liege, 1930. Burnham Bucks: Plainsong and Mediaeval Music Society, [1930]
KONGRESS 1936	Congres de la Societat Internacional de Musicologica a Barcelona, 1936
KONGRESS 1937	Atti del Secondo congresso internazionale de Musica, Firenze-Cremona, 1937 (1940)
KONGRESS 1939	Papers Read at the International Congress of Musicology, New York, 1939
KONGRESS 1952	Fünfter Kongress der Internationalen Gesellschaft für Musikwissenschaft, Utrecht, (1953)
KONGRESS 1956	Bericht über der Internationalen Musikwissenschaftlichen Kongress, Wien, 1956
KONGRESS 1958	Bericht über den siebenten Internationalen Musikwissenschaftlichen Kongress Köln, 1956. Kassel: Bärenreiter, 1959

Abbreviations

KONGRESS 1961	Report of the Eighth Congress New York, 1961. Kassel: Bärenreiter, 1961
KONGRESS 1967	Report of the Tenth Congress, Ljubljana, 1967
LSJ	Lute Society Journal (London)
MD	Musica Disciplina
Mf	Die Musikforschung
MfM	Monatshefte für Musikgeschichte
MGG	Die Musik in Geschichte und Gegenwart, edited by F. Blume, 14 vols., Kassel: Bärenreiter Verlag, 1949-1967
M&L	Music and Letters
MLQ	Modern Language Quarterly
MMR	Monthly Musical Record
MQ	Musical Quarterly
MT	Musical Times
n.d.	no date
NOHM	New Oxford History of Music
NOTES	Quarterly Journal of the Music Library Association
n.p.	no place
NYPL	New York Public Library
ÖMZ	Österreichische Musikzeitschrift
OvKNTV	Orgaan van de Koninklijke Nederlandsche Toonkunstnaars-Vereeniging
PRMA	Proceedings of the Royal Musical Association
RB	Revue Belge de Musicologie
RIM	Rivista Italiana de Musicologica
RM	Revue Musicale
RMA	Royal Musical Association, Research Chronicles
RMI	Rivista Musicale Italiana
RMl	Revue de Musicologie
RMM	Record and Music Magazine
SIMG	Sammelbände der Internationalen Musikgesellschaft

Abbreviations

SMZ	Schweizerische Musikzeitung
STMf	Svensk Tidning för Musikforskning
SzMw	Studien zur Musikwissenschaft
transl.	translated, translator
TVNMg	Tijdschrift der Vereeniging van Nederlandsche Musiekgeschiedenis
VfMw	Vierteljahrschrift für Musikwissenschaft
ZfdG	Zeitschrift für die Gitarre
ZfIb	Zeitschrift für Instrumentenbau
ZfM	Zeitschrift für Musik
ZfMw	Zeitschrift für Musikwissenschaft
ZIMG	Zeitschrift der Internationalen Musikgesellschaft

BIBLIOGRAPHY

BOETTICHER, Wolfgang, ed. *Handschriftlich überlieferte Lauten- und*   **1**
Gitarren-tabulaturen des 16. bis 18. Jahrhunderts. (RISM B VII)
Munchen: G. Henle Verlag, forthcoming.

Breitkopf Supplemento IV dei Catalogi. Leipzig, 1769. [Tablature   **2**
incipits to 66 Partite by Weiss.]

BRENET, Michel. "La Libraire musicale en France de 1653-à 1790   **3**
d'après les registres de privilege," *SIMG* VIII (1906-1907): 401-66.

BROWN, Howard M. *Instrumental Music Printed Before 1600: A*   **4**
Bibliography. Cambridge, Mass.: Harvard University Press, 1965.

DAY, Cyrus L. and Eleanore B. Murrie. "English Song-Books, 1651-1702,   **5**
and Their Publishers," *The Library* 4th ser. XVI/4 (1936): 355-401.

————. *English Song-Books, 1651-1702, a Bibliography of Firstline*   **6**
Index of Songs. London: Bibliographical Society, 1937. 439p.

DOUGHTIE, Edward. *Lyrics from English Airs, 1596-1622.* Cambridge,   **7**
Mass.: Harvard University Press, 1970.

LESURE, François and G. Thibault. *Bibliographie des éditions d'Adrian*   **8**
LeRoy et Robert Ballard (1551-1598). Paris: Société Française
de Musicologie, 1955.

————. "Bibliographie des éditions musicales publiées par Nicolas   **9**
Du Chemin," *AnnMl* I (1953): 269-73.

POHLMANN, Ernst. *Laute, Theorbe, Chitarrone. Die Instrumente, ihre*   **10**
Musik und Literatur von 1500 bis zur Gegenwart. Bremen:

17

Veröffentlichung des Archivs "Deutsche Musikpflege," 1968, rev. ed. 1971. 416p.

11   PURCELL, Ronald C. *Classic Guitar, Lute, and Vihuela Discography.* New York: Belwin-Mills Music Pub. Co., 1976. 117p.

12   *Versteigerung der Musikbibliothek des Herrn Dr. Werner Wolfheim . . . durch die Firmen: M. Breslauer und L. Leipmanssohn.* Berlin, 1928-1929. Vol. I: pp. 29-41; Vol. II: pp. 196, 206-20.

13   ZUTH, Josef. *Handbuch der Laute und Gitarre.* Wien: Verlag der Zeitschrift für die Gitarre, 1926. 297p.

See also: 26, 29, 188, 313, 544; Pruitt, **909, 910, 962, 1524.**

CITTERN

14   Anon. "English Cittern Music," *GSJ* VI (1953): 112-13.

15   ABBOTT, Djilda and Ephraim Segerman. *The Cittern in England Before 1700.* Manchester: Northern Renaissance Instruments. Report no. 1, 1974.

16   BYLER, A. "The Music for Cittern and Gittern in the Mulliner Book," *JAMS* V (1952): 142.

17   CHARNASSÉ, Hélène. "Sur la transcription des recueils de cistre édités par Adrian LeRoy et Robert Ballard (1564-1565)," *RMI* 49 (1963): 184-202.

18   DANNER, Peter. "Dd.4.23 or English Cittern Music Revisited," *JLSA* III (1970): 1-12.

19   DART, Thurston. "The Cittern and Its English Music," *GSJ* I (1948): 46-63.

20   DENIJS, S. B. V. "Cithermakers te Amsterdam in het begin den zeventiende eeuw," *CdM* VI (1934): 67ff.

21   DEVOTO, Daniel. "Métamorphoses d'une cithare," *RMI* 41 (1958): 27-37.

FORTUNE, Nigel. "An Italian Arch-Cittern," *GSJ* V (1952):43. **22**

GUICHARD, L. "Le cistre de Rousseau," *RMl* 50 (1964):229-31. **23**

HADAWAY, Robert. "The Cittern," *EM* I/2 (1973):77-80. **24**

REINHARD, Kurt. "Cister," *MGG* 1451-58. **25**

TYLER, James. "Checklist of Music for the Cittern," *EM* II/1 (1974): **26**
25-29.

VOIGT, A. Die Cithern (Citole, Cittern, Cithren, Cythren, Citharn, **27**
Cither, Cistre etc.) *Deutsche Instrumente-Bauzeitung* 37 (1936):
131ff.

WALDBAUER, Ivan. *The Cittern in the Sixteenth Century and Its Music* **28**
in France and the Low Countries. Unpublished Ph.D. diss., Harvard,
1964. 435+41p.

WEIGAND, George A. "The Cittern Repertoire," *EM* I (1973):81-83. **29**

WINTERNITZ, Emanuel. "The Survival of the Kithara and the Evolution **30**
of the Cittern," *Journal of the Warburg Institute* XXIV (1961):
222-29.

See also: 506, 1052, 1075, 1117: pp. 489-91, 1684, 1699.

COMPOSERS / PERFORMERS—GENERAL BIOGRAPHY

BALFOORT, Dirk J. *Het Muziekleven in Nederland, 1600-1800.* **31**
Amsterdam, 1938.

BROSSARD, Yolande de. *Musiciens de Paris 1535-1792, actes d'état civil* **32**
d'après Le Fichier Laborde de la bibliothèque nationale. Vie musicale
en France sous les Rois Bourbons. Paris: Picard, 1965.

CHILESOTTI, Oscar. "Note circa alcuni liutisti italiana della prima metá **33**
del cinquecento," *RMl* IX (1902):36-61.

DART, Thurston. "English Music and Musicians in 17th-Century Holland," **34**
KONGRESS 1952, pp. 139-45.

35 ECORECHEVILLE, Jules. *Actes d'état-civil de musiciens insinués au Châtelet de Paris (1539-1650)*. Paris, 1907.

36 HAMMOND, Frederick. "Musicians at the Medici Court in the Mid-Seventeenth Century," *AMu* (1974), pp. 151-69.

37 JURGENS, Madeleine. *Documents du Minutier Central (1600-1650)*. Vol. I. Paris: S. E. V. P. E. N., 197-. pp. 266-75, 461-70.

38 KASTNER, Santiago. *Contribución al estudio de la musica española y portugesa*. Lisbon: Editorial Atica, Ida, 1941. 378p.

39 LA LAURENCIE, Lionel de. *Les luthistes*. Paris: Henri Laurens, 1928.

40 LUIZZI, F. *I Musicisti in Francia*. Rome: Edizione d'Arte Danesi, 1946. 329p

41 NAGEL, Wilibald. "Zur Geschichte der Music am Hofe von Darmstadt," *MfM* 32 (1900):1ff.

42 PANUFNIK, Tomasz. Lutnictow polski—Der Polnische Lauten- und Geigenbau," *Muzyka* I (1950):42-47.

43 PRAT, Marsal D. *Diccionario biografico, bibliografico, historic, critico de guitarras . . . guitarristas*. Buenos Aires: Romero y Fernandez, 1934. 468p.

44 SELFRIDGE-FIELD, Eleonor. "Annotated Membership Lists of the Venetian Instrumentalists Guild, 1672-1727," *RMA* 9 (1971):1-52.

45 SPINK, Ian. "The Musicians of Queen Henrietta-Maria: Some Notes and References in the English State Papers," *AMl* 36 (1964):177-82.

46 SZULC, Z. *Słownik lutników Polskich*. Posen: Tow. Przyg. Nauk, 1953.

47 TERZI, Bruno. *Dizionario dei chitarristi e liutai italiani*. Bologna, 1937. 286p.

48 WAGNER, Rudolf. "Wilhelm Breitengraser und die Nürnberger Kirchen- und Schulmusik seiner Zeit," *Mf* (1949), pp. 168-70.

See also: 891, 898, 900, 901, 907, 929, 976, 1172, 1192, 1196, 1197, 1223.

COMPOSERS / PERFORMERS—INDIVIDUAL BIOGRAPHY

ABEL, John (1654-1724)

FARMER, Henry G. "A King's Musician for the Lute and Voice,   **49**
John Abel (1654-1724)," *Hinrichsen's Music Book* VII (1952):
445-56.

ABONDANTE, Giulio (fl. 1550's)

EITNER, Robert. "Giulio Abondantes Lautenbücher," *MfM*   **50**
VIII (1876): 119-21.

ADRIANSEN, Emanuel (1550- ?)

HAMBURGER, Povl. "Die Fantasien in Emanuel Adriansens   **51**
Pratum Musicum (1600)," *ZfMw* XII (1929-1930): 148-60.

SPIESSENS, Godelieve. "Emmanuel Adrianssen et Son Pratum   **52**
Musicum," *AMl* XXXVI (1964): 142-51.

————. *Het Pratum Musicum von Adriaensen, Antwerpen, 1600.*   **53**
Unpublished Lizenziatsschrift, Universität Löwen, 1957.
[Published as *Luitmuziek van Emanuel Adriaensen.* Monumenta
Musicae Belgicae, X, Antwerp, 1966.]

AGRICOLA, Martin (1486-1556)

HALLOWAY, William W. *Martin Agricola's instrumentalis deudsch:*   **54**
A Translation. Unpublished Ph.D., North Texas State University,
1972. 246p.

ALBERTO da Rippe (fl. 1550's). *See also:* 1651.

BUGGERT, Robert W. *Alberto da Ripa: Lutenist and Composer.*   **55**
Unpublished Ph.D. diss., University of Michigan, 1956. 440p.
UMOO-21154.

PROD'HOMME, Jacques-G. "Guillaume Morlaye, éditeur d'Albert   **56**
de Ripe, luthiste et bourgeois de Paris," *RMl* VI (1925): 157-67.

PRUNIERES, Henri. *L'opera italien en France avant Lully.* Paris,   **57**
1913. XVI-XIX.

ROLLIN, Monique. "Alberto da Rippe," *MGG* 11:549-50.   **58**

59 TIERSOT, J. "Ronsard et la musique de son temps," *SIMG* IV (1902-1903): 70-73.

60 VACCARO, Jean-Michel M. *Les fantaisies pour luth d'Albert de Rippe.* Unpublished Ph.D., Université de Tours, 1968. 2 vols.

ALBRECHTSBERGER, Johann Georg (1736-1809). *See also:* **1538.**

60a GOOS, Herta. "Albrechtsberger, J. G.," *MGG* 1:303-307.

ALEMANUS, Johannes Maria. *See:* **357, 358.**

ALLEGRI, Lorenzo

61 GHISI, Federico. "Ballet Entertainment in Pitti Palace, Florence, 1608-1625," *MQ* XXXV/3 (1949): 421-36.

ALLISON, Richard (fl. 1600). *See also:* **1021.**

62 ANDERSON, Ronald E. *Richard Allison's Psalter (1599) and Devotional Music in England to 1640.* Unpublished Ph.D. diss., University of Iowa, 1975. 724p. [incl. Psalmes of David].

AMAT, Juan Carlos (1572-1642)

63 PUJOL, Emilio. "Significación de Joan Carlos Amat (1572-1642) en la historia de la guitarra," *AnM* V (1950): 125-46.

64 SUBIRÁ, José. "Carles y Amat," *MGG* 1:401-402.

ANERIO, Felice (1560-1614)

65 FELLERER, Gustav. "Anerio, Felice," *MGG* 1:470-74, 16:215.

ATTAIGNANT, Pierre (d. 1553). *See also:* **1423.**

66 FEDOROV, V. "Attaignant, Pierre," *MGG* 1:766-70.

67 HEARTZ, Daniel. *Pierre Attaignant, Royal Printer of Music: a Historical Study and Bibliographical Catalogue.* Berkeley and Los Angeles, University of California Press, 1969. 451p.

68 LESURE, François. "Pierre Attaignant notes et documents," *MD* III (1949): 33-40.

YONG, Kwee Him. "A New Source of Prelude 1 in Attaignant's   **69**
Tres breve et familiere introduction," *TVNMg* XXI/4 (1970):
211-24.

BACH, Johann Sebastian (1685-1750)

ARTZT, Alice. "The Third Lute Suite by Bach," *JLSA* I   **70**
(1968):9-14.

BACHA, ———. "Une suite pour luth de J. Seb. Bach," *Le*   **71**
Guide Musicale no. 6-7 (1913).

BECKER, Carl F. "Die g-moll Lautenfuge von Joh. Seb. Bach,"   **72**
Die Hausmusik in 16. bis 18. Jahrhunderte. Leipzig: Fest, 1840.

BRUGER, Hans D. "Bachs Verhältnis zur Laute," *Die Laute*   **73**
II (1920-1921).

DOMBOIS, Eugen M. "The Allegro from J. S. Bach's Prelude,   **74**
Fugue and Allegro in E flat Major BWV 998," *LSJ* XIV
(1972):25-28.

———. "Über die Fuge und das Prélude aus Johann Sebastian   **75**
Bachs Präludium, Fuge und Allegro Es-dur BWV 998," *LSJ*
XV (1973):37-46.

FERGUSON, Howard. "Bach's Lauten-Werck," *M&L* 48   **76**
(1967):259-64.

GIESBERT, Franz J. "Bach und die Laute," *Mf* 25 (1972):485-88.   **77**

KOHLHASE, Thomas. *Johann Sebastian Bachs Kompositionen*   **78**
für Lauteninstrumente. Kritische Edition mit Untersuchungen
zur überlieferung, Besetzung und Spielteknik. Unpublished
Ph.D., University of Tubingen, 1972. 247p.

NEEMANN, Hans. "Johann Sebastian Bachs Lauten-   **79**
Kompositionen," *Bach Jahrbuch* XXVIII (1931):14-27.

RADKE, Hans. "War Joh. Seb. Bach Lautenspieler?" *Festschrift*   **80**
ENGEL pp. 281-89.

SCHULZE, Hans-J. "Wer intavolierte Johann Sebastian Bachs   **81**
Lauten-Kompositionen?," *Mf* XIX (1966):32-39.

TAPPERT, Wilhelm. "Johann Sebastian Bachs Kompositionen   **82**
für die Laute," *MfM* X (1901):36-40.

83   WADE, Graham. "Bach and the Classic Guitar," *Guitar News* 97 (January-February): 13, 14.

BAÏF, Jean Antoine (1533-1589)

84   WALKER, G. P. "Baïf, Jean Antoine," *MGG* 1:1084-86.

BAKFARK, Valentin (1507-1576)

85   CHYBINSKI, Adolf. "Bakfark," *Mysl. Mus. Kattowitz* (1918), p. 7ff.

86   ———. "Bakfark," *Przeglad Muzyczny* VI (1918): 1 ff.

87   CSIKI, J. "Bakfark," *Magyr Könyvszemle* (1905), p. 116ff.

88   GOMBOSI, Otto. "Bakfark," *MGG* 1:1092-95.

89   ———. Bakfark Bálint élete és muvei [=Bakfark, Leben und Werke 1507-1575]. *Musicologica Hungarica* II (1935).

90   ———. *Der Lautenist Valentin Bakfark Leben und Werke (1507-1575)*. Zoltan Falvy (ed.). Budapest: Akademiai Kiadó. 1967.

91   HARASZTI, Emile. "Un grand luthiste du XVIe siècle: Valentin Bakfark," *RMl* X (1929): 159-76.

92   KAISER, Ludwig. *Valentin Greff-Bakfark.* Unpublished Ph.D. diss., Wien, 1907.

93   KLEIN, Karl K. "Der Lautenist Valentin Greff-Bakfark (1507-1576)," *Siedenburger aus der Statt Kron Siedenburg Vierteljahrschrift* 59, pp. 114-18.

94   OPIENSKI, Henryk. "Sześć listow lutnisty Bekwarka," *Kwartalnik Muzyczny* VI (1930): 158ff.

95   ———. *Valentin Bakfark.* Unpublished Ph.D. diss., Leipzig, 1914.

96   ———. "Valentin Bakfark, lutinista," *Biblioteka Warszawska* II (1906): 46ff.

97   POLINSKI, Alexander. "Bakfark," *Echo Muzyczne* (1887), p. 378ff.

BALLARD, Robert, Sr. (?-1588)

98   FEDOROV, V. "Ballard, Robert," *MGG* 1:1142-56.

BALLARD, Robert, Jr. (1575-1650). *See also:* 7, 17.

24

BRENET, Michel. "Le Luthiste Robert Ballard," *Le Guide*   **99**
Musical (1893).

PRUNIÈRES, Henri. "Documents pour servir à la biographie des   **100**
luthistes R. Ballard et F. Pinel," *SIMG* XV (1913-1914): 587-90.

ROLLIN, Monique. "Ballard, Robert," *MGG* 15:438-39.   **101**

BALLET, William (fl. 1600). *See:* **1492.**

BALLETTI, Bernardino (fl. 1550)

VAN DER STRAETEN, Edmund. "Balletti, Bernardino,"   **102**
Grove I:394.

BANCHIERI, Adriano (1567-1634)

REDLICH, H. F. "Banchieri, Adriano," *MGG* 1:1206-12.   **103**

BANISTER, John (d. 1679)

WESTRUP, Jack A. "Banister, John," *MGG* 1:1212-13.   **104**

BARBERIS, Melchior de (fl. 1540). *See also:* **1446.**

BOETTICHER, Wolfgang. "Barberis, Melchior de," *MGG*   **105**
1:1234-35.

ECHOLES, Jane A. *Melchior de Barberis' Lute Intabulations of*   **106**
Sacred Music. Unpublished Master's thesis, University of
North Carolina, 1973. 275p.

BARBETTA, Giulio (1540-1603)

BOETTICHER, Wolfgang. "Barbetta, Giulio," *MGG* 1:1238-42.   **107**

THOMAS, Benjamin W. *The Lute Books of Giulio Barbetta: A*   **108**
Polyphonic Transcription of the Composer's Complete Works
and an Analysis of the Fourteen Fantasias. Unpublished Ph.D.
diss., North Texas State University, 1973. 4 vols.

BARLEY, William (fl. 1600). *See also:* **1523.**

WARD, John. "Barley's Songs Without Words," *LSJ* XII (1970):   **109**
5-22.

Composers / Performers—Individual Biography

BARON, Ernst Gottlieb (1696-1760)

110 BOETTICHER, Wolfgang. "Baron, Ernst G.," *MGG* 1:1338-40.

111 SMITH, Douglas Alton. "Baron and Weiss Contra Mattheson: In Defense of the Lute," *JLSA* VI (1973):48-62.

BASSET, Jehan (fl. 1630)

112 LA LAURENCIE, Lionel de. "Un maitre de luth au XVIIe siècle: Jehan Basset et le luthiste Jacques Gaultier," *RM* (1923), pp. 224-37.

BATAILLE, Gabriel (1575-1630). *See also:* 1419.

113 LESURE, François. "Bataille, Gabriel," *MGG* 1:1402-1404.

114 ———. "Documents inédite relatifs au luthiste Gabriel Bataille," *RMI* (1947), pp. 72-88.

115 VERCHALY, André. "Gabriel Bataille et son oeuvre personelle pour chant et luth," *RMI* (1947), pp. 1-24.

BATCHELAR, Daniel (fl. 1600). *See also:* 1458.

116 DOUGHTIE, E. "Sidney, Tessier, Batchelar and a Musicall Banquet: Two Notes," *Renaissance News* XVIII/2 (1965):123-26.

BATESON, Thomas (1570-1630)

117 CUTTS, John P. "Everie Woman in Her Humor," *Renaissance News* XVIII/3 (1965):209-13.

BENTIVOGLIO, Ascanio (fl. 1630?). *See:* 1506.

BESARD, Jean-Baptiste (1567-1625). *See also:* 129, 1416, 1417, 1455, 1520.

118 BAILLE, L. "Jean Baptiste Besard, Luthiste Bisontin," *Revue de Franche-Comté* (15 February, 1925).

119 BOETTICHER, Wolfgang. "Besardus," *MGG* 1:1815-19.

120 CASTAN, Auguste. "Note sur Jean-Baptiste Besard de Besancon célèbre luthiste." *Mémoires de la société d'émulation du Doubs*, ser. 5, I (1876):25-32.

26

CHILESOTTI, Oscar. "Di Giovani Battista Besardo e del suo   **121**
Thesaurus Harmonicus," *Gazetta Musicale* (1886).

————. "Musiciens français: Jean Baptiste Besard, et les luthistes   **122**
du XVIe siècle," *Congrès international d'histoire de la musique,*
1900: Documents, mémoires et voeux. Solemes, 1901, pp. 179-
90. [Also in *Revue d'Histoire et de Critique Musicale*, March
1901.]

GARTON, Joseph N. *J-B Besard's Thesaurus Harmonicus.*   **123**
Unpublished Ph.D. diss., Indiana University, 1952.

SUTTON, Julia. *Jean Baptiste Besard's Novus Partus of 1617.*   **124**
Unpublished Ph.D. diss., Eastman School of Music, Rochester,
1962.

————. "Jean-Baptise Besard, Renaissance Gentleman," *JLSA*   **125**
I (1968): 1-8.

BÉTHUNE, Michel de (fl. 1660)

LA LAURENCIE, Lionel de. "Quelques luthistes françiase du   **126**
XVIIe siècle, Michel de Béthune, les Du But et René
Mesangeau," *RMI* 8 (1923): 145-55.

BIANCHINI, Domenico (fl. 1540)

MORCOURT, Richard de. "Le Livre de Tablature de Luth de   **127**
Domenico Bianchini, 1546," in *La Musique Instrumentale de*
la Renaissance, edited by J. Jacquot. Paris: CNRS, 1955,
pp. 179-95.

BITTNER (Büttner) Jacques (fl. 1670)

RAVE, Wallace. [Pieces de lut] by Jacques Bittner. (A Baroque   **128**
Lute Tablature dated 1682, edited by W. J. Rave.) Unpublished
Master's thesis, University of Illinois, Urbana, 1965.

BOCQUET, Charles (fl. 1600)

LA LAURENCIE, Lionel de. "Les Luthistes Charles Bocquet,   **129**
Antoine Francisque et Jean-Baptiste Besard," *RMI* (1926),
pp. 69-77, 126-33.

BOESSET, Pierre (1586-1643). *See:* **1419.**

129a ALDERMAN, Pauline. *Antoine Boesset and the Air de Cour.* Ph.D. University of Southern California, 1946. 248p.

BONO, Pietro (fl. 1480)

130 HARASZTI, Emile. "Les Musciens de Mathias Corvin et de Béatrice D'Aragon," in *La Musique Instrumentale de la Renaissance*, edited by J. Jacquot. Paris: CNRS, 1955, pp. 35-59.

131 ———. "Pietro Bono luthiste de Mathias Corvin," *RMI* 28 (1949): 73-85.

132 LOCKWOOD, Lewis. "Pietrobono and the Instrumental Tradition at Ferrara in the Fifteenth Century," *RIM* X (1975): 115-33.

BORRONO, Pietro P. (fl. 1560). *See:* **1516.**

BOSSINENSIS, Franciscus (fl. 1500)

133 DARDO, G. "Bossinensis, Franciscus," *MGG* 15:983-85.

134 DISERTORI, Benvenuto. *Le Frottole Per Canto e Liuto Intabulate da Franciscus Bossinensis.* Milan: G. Ricordi, 1964. Vol. 3.

135 SARTORI, Claudio. "A Little-Known Petrucci Publication; 'The Second Book of Lute Tablatures' by Francesco Bossinensis," *MQ* XXXIV (1948): 234-45.

BOTTEGARI, Cosimo (1554- ?)

136 MacCLINTOCK, Carol. *The Bottegari Lutebook.* Ph.D. diss., Wellesly College, 1965.

137 ———. "A Court Musician's Songbook: Modena MS C 311," *JAMS* IX (1956): 177-92.

BRADE, Christian (fl. 1620). *See:* **233.**

BRAYSSING, Gregoire (fl. 1550). *See also:* **951.**

138 LESURE, François. "Brayssing, Gregoire," *MGG* 2:22-24.

BRICEÑO, Luis (fl. 1626). *See also:* **1473.**

CHARNASSÉ, Hélène. "A propos d'un récent article sur la   **139**
méthode pour la guitare de Luis Briceño," *RMl* 52 (1966):204-
207.

LESURE, François. "Trois instrumentistes française du XVIIe   **140**
siècle," *RMl* 37 (1955):186-87.

SUBIRÁ, José. "Briceño, Luis," *MGG* 2:318-19.   **141**

BRIGA, (Arriga, Brigadi) Bartolomeo. *See:* **44**.

BRONIKOWSKY, (Bogislaus Stanislaus?) de (fl. 1740). *See:* **703**.

BROSSARD, Sebastian de (1650-1730)

LEBEAU, E. "Brossard, Sebastian de," *MGG* 2:333-37.   **142**

————. "L'entrée de la collection musicale de Sebastien   **143**
de Brossard à la Bibliothèque du Roi, d'aprés des documents
inédites," *RMl* (1950), pp. 78-93; (1951), pp. 20-43.

BRUHNS, Paul (1612-1655)

KÖLSCH, Heinz. "Bruhns, Paul," in article "Bruhns, Nicolas,"   **144**
MGG 2:395-96.

CABEZON, Antonio (1510-1566)

ANGLÉS, Higini. "Cabezon, Antonio," *MGG* 2:596-604.   **145**

CACCINI, Giulio (1550-1610)

GHISI, Federico. "Caccini, Giulio," *MGG* 2:609-12.   **146**

JOINER, M. "Caccini's 'Amarilli mia bella'-its Influence on   **147**
Miserere My Maker," *LSJ* X (1968):6-14.

MYERS, Joan. "Caccini-Dowland: Monody Realized," *JLSA*   **148**
III (1970):22-34.

CALDARA, Antonio (1670-1736)

PAUMGARTNER, Bernhard. "Caldara, Antonio," *MGG* 2:645-50.   **149**

29

CAMPION, François (1686-1748)

150   BORREL, Eugene. "Campion, François," *MGG* 2:728.

CAMPION, Thomas (1567-1620). *See also:* 230, 1167.

151   AUDEN, William H. and John HOLLANDER. *Selected Songs of Thomas Campion.* Boston: David Godine, 1973, pp. 3-29.

152   BARTSTOW, Robert. *The 'Lord Hayes Masque' by Thomas Campion.* Unpublished Ph.D., Ohio State University, 1963. 194p.

153   DART, Thurston. "Campion, Thomas," *MGG* 2:728-29.

154   DAVID, Walter R. "Melodic and Poetic Structure of Campion and Dowland," *Criticism* IV (1962):89-107.

155   ————. "Note on Accent and Quantity in 'A Book of Ayres'," *MLQ* 22 (1961):32-36.

156   ELDRIDGE, Muriel T. *Thomas Campion: His Poetry and Music, 1567-1620. A Study in Relationship.* Unpublished Ph.D. diss., Michigan State University.

157   GODARD, John. "Such Distraction of Musicke. A Note on the Music in the Masque of Thomas Campion," *RMM* 3/7 (1968): 231-33.

158   GREER, David. "Campion the Musician," *LSJ* IX (1967):7-16.

159   HARPER, John. "A New Way of Making Ayres? Thomas Campion: Towards a Revaluation," *MT* vol. 110, no. 1513 (March 1954), pp. 262-63.

160   JOINER, Mary. "Another Campion Song?" *M&L* 48 (1967):138-39.

161   KASTENDIECK, Miles M. *England's Musical Poet, Thomas Campion.* London: Oxford University Press, 1938. 203p.

162   LAWRENCE, W. J. "Notes on a Collection of Masque Music," *M&L* III (1922):49-58.

CAPIROLA, Vincenzo (fl. 1515). *See also:* 1678.

163   CHIESA, Ruggero. "Storia della letteratura del liuto e della chitarra," *IFr* III/11 (April 1975):18-22.

CARRA, M. Marchete (fl. 1520). *See:* 665.

CARDON, Jean-Guillain (1732-1788)

SOREL-NITZBERG, Alice. "Cardon, Jean-Guillain," *MGG*   **164**
2:832-33.

CAROSO, Fabritio

ARKWRIGHT, G. E. P. "Caroso, Fabritio," *Grove* 2:89-90.   **165**

CASTALDI, Bellerophon (1581-1649)

FORTUNE, Nigel. "Castaldi, Bellerophon," *Grove* 2:111.   **166**

CASTRO, Jean de (1540?-1600?)

SCHMIDT-GÖRG, Joseph. "Castro, Jean de," *MGG* 2:904-906.   **167**

VAN DER STRAETEN, Edmund. "Castro, Jean de," *Grove*   **168**
2:117-18.

CATO, Diomedes (1570-1615). *See also:* **218, 1245.**

HALSKI, Czesław R. "Cato, Diomedes," *Grove* 2:709.   **169**

OSOSOTOWICZ, Alena. "Nieznany sześciogłosowy motet i   **170**
utwory organovie Diomedesa Catona z tabulatury
Torunskiej," [The Unknown 6-part Motet and Organ
Work of D. Cato in the Thorner Tablature of 1595.]
Muzyka 4 (1959):45-59.

CAVENDISH, Michael (1565-1628)

ARNOLD, Denis. "Cavendish, Michael," *MGG* 2:937-38.   **171**

CHANCY, François, Sieur de (?-1656)

VERCHALY, André. "Chancy, François, Sieur de," *MGG*   **172**
2:1033-34.

CHARLES, Duc de Croy (1560-1612)

BIRKNER, G. "La tablature de luth de Charles, Duc de Croy et   **173**
d'Archot (1560-1612)," *RMI* (1963), pp. 18-46.

31

CLODIUS

174   NIESSEN, W. *Das Lautenbuch des Leipziger Studenten Clodius.*
Unpublished Ph.D. diss., Berlin, 1891.

COLEMAN, Charles (d. 1664). *See:* 1151.

COLISTA, Lelio (fl. seventeenth century)

175   WESSELY-KROPIK, Helene. *Lelio Colista, ein römischer Meister
vor Corelli; Leben und Umwelt.* Österreichischer Akademie der
Wissenschaften. Vol. 237, no. 4. Vienna, 1961.

CONTI, Francesco B. (1682-1732)

176   PAUMGARTNER, Bernhard. "Conti, Francesco B.," *MGG*
2:1640-43.

177   POHL, Carl F. "Conti, Francesco Bartolomeo," *Grove* 2:414-15.

COPERARIO (Cooper) Giovanni (1570-1626). *See also:* 178, 1144.

178   CHARTERIS, Richard. *John Coperario (Cooper) ca. 1570-1626:
His Life and Music with a Critical Edition of His Complete Works.*
Unpublished Ph.D. diss., University of Canterbury, New Zealand,
forthcoming.

179   ———. "Autography of John Coperario," *M&L* 56 (1975):41-46.

180   DART, Thurston. "Coperario, Giovanni," *MGG* 2:1658-61.

181   ———. "Two English Musicians at Heidelberg in 1613," *MT*
vol. 111 no. 1523 (January), pp. 29, 31-32.

CORBETTA, Francesco (1615-1681)

182   CHILESOTTI, Oscar. "Francesco Corbetta guitarrista," *Gazzetta
Musicale di Milano* XLIX (1888): 386ff.

183   KENNARD, D. "A Note on F. Corbetta and His Tablature," *GR*
9 (1962): 9ff.

184   KIETH, Richard. "La Guitarre Royale," *Recherches sur la musique
française classique* VI (1966): 73-94.

PINNELL, Richard. *The Role of Francesco Corbetta (1615-*   **185**
1681) in the History of Music for the Baroque Guitar,
Including a Transcription of His Complete Works. 2 vols.
Unpublished Ph.D. diss., University of California, Los Angeles,
1976.

SCHULTZ, N. "Francesco Corbetta und das Generalbas-Spieler,"   **186**
Mf 4 (1951): 371-72.

CORKINE, William (fl. 1610)

BOETTICHER, Wolfgang. "Corkine, William," *MGG*   **187**
2:1679-80.

CUTTING, Francis (fl. 1600). *See also:* **117, 118, 233, 1458.**

DART, Thurston. "Cutting, Francis," *Grove* 2:566.   **188**

NEWTON, Richard. "Francis Cutting: A Bibliography," *LSJ*   **189**
I (1959): 38-47.

CYPRIANO de RORE (1516-1565). *See:* **1457.**

DALZA, Joan Ambrosio (fl. 1500). *See also:* **1511, 1517.**

CHARLTON, Katherine. *The Lute Music of Joan Ambrosio*   **190**
Dalza. Master's thesis, California State University, Fullerton,
forthcoming.

CHIESA, Ruggero. "Storia della letteratura del liuto e della   **191**
chitarra," *IFr* no. 5 (October, 1973): 15-20.

SNOW, Robert Joseph. *Petrucci: Intabulatura de Lauto, Libro*   **192**
Primo Joan Ambrosio Dalza. Unpublished Master's thesis,
Indiana University, 1955. 6 + 85p.

DANYEL, John (1564-1625?). *See also:* **1498;** Judd, P. "The Songs of
John Danyel," *M&L* XVII (1936): 118-23.

ARNOLD, Denis. "Danyel, John," *MGG* 2:1892-93.   **193**

LINDLEY, David. "John Danyel's 'Eyes looke no More',"   **194**
LSJ XVI (1974): 9-16.

195   ROOLEY, Anthony. "The Lute Solos and Duets of John Danyel," *LSJ* XIII (1971): 18-27.

196   SCOTT, David. "John Danyel: His Life and Songs," *LSJ* XIII (1971): 7-17.

DAUBE, Johann F. (1733-1797)

197   REICHERT, Georg. "Daube, Johann F.," *MGG* 3:27-29.

DAZA, Esteban (fl. 1570). *See also:* 1473.

198   EVERS, Reinbert. *Die Fantasien aus Esteban Daza's El Parnaso und ihre Stellung in der Entwicklungsgeschichte der Fantasie für Vihuela.* Ph.D. diss., Ruhr-Universität-Bochum, forthcoming.

199   PEDRELL, Felipe. "Quelque commentaires a une lettre de l'insigne Maitre Victoria," *SIMG* II (1909-1910): 473ff.

200   PURCELL, Ronald C. *Esteban Daza, "El Parnaso"*. . . . Unpublished Master's thesis, California State University, Northridge, 1972. 2 vols.

DELAIR, Etienne (1662- ?)

201   LAUNAY, Denise. "Delair, Etienne," *MGG* 3:115.

DELATRE, Claude Petit Jean (?-1589?)

202   VAN DEN BORREN, Charles. "Delatre, Claude Petit Jean," *MGG* 3:122-25.

DENSS, Adrian (fl. 1594)

203   BOETTICHER, Wolfgang. "Denss, Adrian," *MGG* 3:195-97.

204   KLÖCKNER, Dieter. *Das Florilegium des Adrian Denss (Köln 1594). Ein Beitrag zur Geschichte der Lautenmusik am Ende des 16. Jahrhunderts.* Beiträge zur Rheinischen Musikgeschichte. Heft 90. Cologne: Arno Volk Verlag, 1970.

205   LOBAUGH, H. Bruce. "Adrian Denns' Florilegium (1594)," *JLSA* III (1970): 13-21.

—————. *Three German Lute Books: Denss' 'Florilegium',*   **206**
1594; Reymann's 'Noctes Musicae', 1598; Rude's 'Flores
Musicae', 1600. Unpublished Ph.D. diss., Eastman School
of Music, 1968. 2 vols. UM 68-13,806.

DENTICE, Fabritio (fl. 1600)

DELLA CORTE, Andrea, "Dentice, Fabritio," *MGG*   **207**
3:197-99.

DES PREZ, Josquin (1440-1521)

YONG, Kwee Him. "Sixteenth-Century Printed Instrumental   **208**
Arrangements of Works by Josquin des Pres. An Inventory,"
TVNMg XXII/1 (1971):43-66.

DIESEL, Nathanael (d. 1744)

LYONS, David B. *The Guitar Music of Nathanael Diesel,*   **209**
Lutenist to the Royal Danish Court, 1736-1744. An
Analysis and Transcription of the Duets. Unpublished
Master's thesis, California State University, Northridge,
1974. 415p.

—————. "Nathanael Diesel, Guitar Tutor to a Royal Lady,"   **210**
JLSA VIII (1975):80-94.

RASMUSSEN, Knud. "Nathanael Diesels guitarkom-   **211**
positioner," *Dansk Aarbog for Musik Forskning* (1963),
pp. 27-68.

D'INDIA, Sigismondo (1580?-1629)

FORTUNE, Nigel. "Italian Secular Monody from 1600 to   **212**
1635," *MQ* 39 (1953):171-95.

—————. "Sigismondo d'India, An Introduction to His Life   **213**
and Works," *PRMA* (1954-1955), pp. 29-47.

MOMPELLIO, Federico. "D'India, Sigismondo," *MGG*   **214**
6:1135-40.

—————. "Sigismondo d'India et il suo primo libro di   **215**
Musiche da cantar sol," *Collectanae Historicae Musicae* I,
pp. 113-34.

DIX, Aureus (1669-1719). *See also:* 273.

216   VOGL, Emil. "Aureus Dix und Antoni Eckstein, zwei Prager Lautenisten," *Mf* XVII (1964): 41-45.

DŁUGORAI, Adalbert (1550- ?)

217   BOETTICHER, Wolfgang. "Długorai, Adalbert," *MGG* 3:615-17.

218   JACHIMECKI, Z. "Lutnisci: Wojciech Długorai, Diomedes Cato, Jacob Połak." *Wpływy Włoskie W Muzyce Polskiej Tl. r 1540-1640.* Krakow, 1911, p. 120ff.

DOWLAND, John (1562-1626). *See also:* 117, 154,   '15-16, 1169, 1171, 1458, 1496, 1501, 1505.

219   BARCLAY-SQUIRE, William. "John Dowland," *MT* 52 (1896): 37ff.

220   ———. "John Dowland," *MT* (February 1897), p. 92ff.

221   ———. "John Dowland," *Gentleman's Magazine* (1906), pp. 287-91.

222   BECKER, Carl. F. *Die englischen Madrigalisten W. Byrd, T. Morley und John Dowland.* Unpublished Ph.D. diss., Bonn, 1901.

223   BROWN, Patricia. "Influences on the Early Lute Songs of John Dowland," *Musicology* (Australia) III (1968-1969): 21-33.

224   DART, Thurston. "John Dowland," *MGG* 3:717-22.

225   ———. "John Dowland and His Music," *The Listener* no. 1264 (1963), p. 858ff.

226   DOUGHTIE, Edward. "Nicholas Breton and Two Songs by Dowland," *Renaissance News* XVII (1964): 1-3.

227   ———. *Poems from the Songbooks of John Dowland.* Unpublished Ph.D. diss., Harvard University, 1963.

228   DOWLING, M. "The Printing of John Dowland's 'Second Book of Songs or Ayres'," *The Library* 4th ser. XII (1932-1933): 365-90.

229   FELLOWES, Edmund H. "The Songs of Dowland," *PRMA* LVI (1929-1930): 1-26.

230   FLOOD, William H. G. "Irish Ancestry of Garland, Dowland, Campion and Purcell," *M&L* III (1922): 59-65.

231   ———. "New Facts about John Dowland," *Gentleman's Magazine* (1906), pp. 287-91.

36

GOINS, Eddie T. *John Dowland and the Art Song.*   **232**
Unpublished Ph.D. diss., University of Iowa, 1962. 167p.

HAMMERICH, Angul. "Musical Relations Between England   **233**
and Denmark in the Seventeenth Century," *SIMG* 13
(1911-1912): 114-19.

HENNING, Rudolf. "A Possible Source of Lachrimae?"   **234**
LSJ XIV (1974): 65-67.

HESELTINE, Philip. "More Light of John Dowland," *MT*   **235**
LXVII (August, 1927): 689-91.

HILL, Cecil. "John Dowland: Some New Facts and a   **236**
Quartercentenary Tribute," *MT* CIV (November, 1963):
785-86.

————. "Dowland," *MT* (March, 1964), p. 199.   **237**

JOHNSON, Francis. "Printer's 'Copy Books' and the Black   **238**
Market in the Elizabethan Book Trade," *The Library* 5th
ser. I (1946): 97-105.

KLESSMAN, Eckart. "Die Deutschlandreisen John   **239**
Dowlands," *Musica* XI (1957): 13-15.

————. "John Dowland," *Hausmusik* 13 (1959): 10-14.   **240**

————. "Die Italienreise John Dowlands," *Musica* XI   **241**
(1957): 320-22.

————. "Die Letzten Jahre John Dowlands," *Musica* XII   **242**
(1958): 390-94.

LOWINSKI, E. *Tonality and Atonality in Sixteenth-Century*   **243**
Music. Berkeley and Los Angeles: University of
California Press, 1961, pp. 54-61.

MANNING, Rosemary. "Lachrimae. A Study of John   **244**
Dowland," *M&L* MLXXV (1944): 44-53.

MIES, Otto. "Dowland's Lachrymae Tune," *MD* IV   **245**
(1950): 59-64.

————. *John Dowland, Leben und Werke.* Unpublished   **246**
Ph.D. diss., Kiel, 1939.

NAGEL, Wilibald. "John Douland's Necessarie Observations   **247**
belonging to lute-playing," (German translation of and
commentary on R. Dowland's *Varietie . . . .(1610) MfM*
XXIII (1891): 145-62.

248   PANUM, Hortense. "Dowland: Christian Den 4Des Galliarde,"
      Aarbok for Musik (Kopenhagen) II (1923): 40-50.

249   POULTON, Diane. "The Burial of John Dowland," *LSJ* IV
      (1962): 32.

250   ———. "Captain Digory Piper of the Sweepstake," *LSJ* IV
      (1962): 17-22.

251   ———. "Dowland's Songs and Their Instrumental Forms," *MMR*
      LXXXI (1959): 175-80.

252   ———. *John Dowland*. London: Faber, 1973. 520p.

253   ———. "John Dowland," *MT* (April, 1964), pp. 275-76.

254   ———. "John Dowland, a Reply to Hill . . . ." *MT* (January, 1964),
      pp. 25-26.

255   ———. "John Dowland and Elizabethan Melancholy," *RMM*
      4 (1969): 40-42.

256   ———. "John Dowland, Doctor of Music," *Consort* XX (1963):
      189-97.

257   ———. "John Dowland's Patron's and Friends," *LSJ* IV (1963):
      7-17.

258   ———. "Lady Hunsden's Puffe," *MT* (July, 1964), p. 518.

259   ———. "The Lute Music of John Dowland," *Consort* VIII (1950):
      10-15.

260   ———. "Was John Dowland a Singer?" *LSJ* VI (1965): 32-37.

261   RICHARDSON, Brian. "New Light on Dowland's Continental
      Movements," *MMR* XC (1960): 3ff.

262   ROOLEY, Anthony. "John Dowland and English Lute Music,"
      EM 3/2 (1975): 115-18.

263   SMITH, James G. *John Dowland: A Reappraisal of His Ayres.*
      Unpublished D.M.A., University of Illinois-Urbana, 1973.
      457p. UM 74-5703.

264   SWAN, A. J. "John Dowland," *GR* 9 (1949): 13.

DOWLAND, Robert (1585-1641). *See also:* **148, 247.**

265   BARCLAY-SQUIRE, William. "Robert Dowland's 'Musical Banquet'
      1610," *Musical Antiquary* I (1909-1910): 45-55.

DART, Thurston. "Dowland, Robert," *MGG* 3:723-24.   **266**

POULTON, Diane. "Some Corrections to the Three Spanish   **267**
Songs in 'A Musicall Banquet'," *LSJ* III (1961):22-26.

DRUSINA, Benedictus de (fl. 1550)

BOETTICHER, Wolfgang. "Drusina, Benedictus de," *MGG*   **268**
3:830-32.

DU BUT (Family) (fl. seventeenth century). *See also:* **126.**

VERCHALY, André. "Du But," *MGG* 3:846-47.   **269**

DU CAURROY, Eustache de (1549-1609)

LESURE, François. "Du Caurroy, Eustache de," *MGG*   **270**
3:850-52.

DU FAUT (fl. 1635)

VERCHALY, André. *MGG* 3:889.   **271**

DU PRE (Du Pre d'Angleterre) (d. 1680?). *See also:* **1183.**

VERCHALY, André. "Du Pre," *MGG* 3:970-71.   **272**

DUVAL, Nicholas. *See:* **1151.**

ECKSTEIN, Antoni (1657-1720). *See also:* **216.**

VOGL, Emil. "Ze životopisu čtyř ceských loutnistů,"   **273**
[towards a biography of Four Bohemian Lutenists].
Z pravy Bertramky 51 (1967):1-9.

EDINTHON, ? *See:* **59.**

EDWARD, Lord Herbert of Cherbury (1582-1648). *See also:* **1169.**

DART, Thurston. "Lord Herbert of Cherbury's Lute Book,"   **274**
M&L XXXVII (1957):136.48.

39

275   LYONS, David B. *Edward, Lord Herbert of Cherbury: His Manuscript. A Study and Edition of the English Lute Solos.* Unpublished Bachelor's thesis, California State University, Northridge, 1973. 227p.

276   POZNIAK, Piotr. "Utwory Polskich lutnistow w rękopisie lorda Herberta of Cherbury," *Z Dziejow Muzyki Polskiej* XV (1971): 27-39.

277   PRICE, Curtis A. "An Organizational Peculiarity of Lord Herbert of Cherbury's Lute-Book," *LSJ* XI (1969): 5-27.

ESPINEL, Vincente (1550- ?)

278   POPE-CONANT, Isabel. "Vincente Espinel as a Musician," *Studies in the Renaissance*, V (1958).

FABRITIUS, Petrus (1587-1651)

279   ENGELKE, B. "Das Lautenbuch des Petrus Fabricus," *Die Heimat* 39 (1929): 265ff.

280   GUDEWILL, Kurt. "Fabritius, Petrus," *MGG* 3:1701-1703.

FALCKENHAGEN, Adam (1697-1761)

281   BOETTICHER, Wolfgang. "Falckenhagen, Adam," *MGG* 3:1743-45.

282   NEEMANN, Hans. "Adam Falckenhagen," *Die Gitarre* VI (1925).

FALCONIERI, Andrea (1586-1656)

283   DEMERINI, Adelmo. "Falconieri, Andrea," *MGG* 3:1740-43.

284   TORCHI, L. *La musica strumentale italiana.* Turin, 1901, pp. 52-53.

FALLERMO, Gabriel (fl. 1580's)

285   BOETTICHER, Wolfgang. "Fallermo, Gabriel," *MGG* 3:1757-58.

FASOLO, Giovanni Battesta (fl. 1659)

286   GHISI, Federico. "Fasolo, Giovanni Battesta," *MGG* 3:1861-62.

FAUNER, J. V.

40

41

296   CHILESOTTI, Oscar. "Perino Fiorentino, liutista del secolo XVIe," *Rivista Fiorentina* I (1908):23ff.

297   WIENANDT, Elwyn A. "Perino Fiorentino and His Lute Pieces," *JAMS* VIII (1955): 2-3.

FLECHA, (Juan) Mateo (1481-1553)

298   ANGLÉS, Higini. "Flecha, (Juan) Mateo," *MGG* 4:292-99.

FLEURY, Francis Nicolas (1630-   ?)

299   VERCHALY, André. "Fleury, Francis Nicolas," *MGG* 4:310-11.

FONTANA, Giovanni Battista (?-1630)

300   GIEGLING, Franz. "Fontana, Giovanni B.," *MGG* 4:496-98.

FORBE, John

301   TERRY, Charles S. "John Forbe's 'Songs and Fancies'," *MQ* XXII (1936):402-19.

FORDE, Thomas (1580-1648)

302   FORTUNE, Nigel. "Forde, Thomas," 4:508-10.

FOSCARINI, Giovanni Paolo

303   DANNER, Peter. "Giovanni Paolo Foscarini and His 'Nuova Inventione'," *JLSA* VII (1974):4-18.

FRANCESCO DA MILANO (1490-1566)   *See also:* **1432.**

304   BARBLAN, Guglielmo. "La vita musicale in Milano nella prima metà del Cinquecento," *Storia di Milano* IX (1961):880-82.

305   CHILESOTTI, Oscar. "Francesco da Milano, liutista della prima metà del secolo XVI," *SIMG* (1902-1903), pp. 382-403.

306   DOREZ, Leon. *La cour du Pape Paul III d'après les registres de la trésorerie secrète.* Paris, 1932. I, pp. 225-32.

————. "Francesco da Milano et la musique du Pape Paul   **307**
III," *La Revue Musicale* XI (1930): 104-13.

GIRAUD, Yves. "Deux livres de tablature inconnus de   **308**
Francesco da Milano," *RMI* LV (1969): 217-19.

GOMBOSI, Otto. "A la recherche de la forme dans la   **309**
musique de la Renaissance: Francesco da Milano," in *La
Musique Instrumenatale de la Renaissance.* Edited by
J. Jacquot. Paris: CNRS, 1955, pp. 165-76.

MERCATI, A. "Favori di Paolo III a musici (Giacomo   **310**
Archadelt-Ivo Barry-Bartolomo Crati-Francesco [Canova]
da Milano) *Note d'Archivo* X (1933): 109-15.

NEWMAN, Joel. "Francesco da Milano," *GR* IX (1949):   **311**
22-23.

————. *Francesco da Milano, a Lutenist of the Sixteenth*   **312**
Century. Unpublished Master's thesis, New York University,
1942.

SLIM, H. Colin. "Francesco Milano: A Bio-bibliographical   **313**
Study," *MD* 18 (1964): 63-84; 19 (1965): 109-28.

WIENANDT, Elwyn A. *Musical Style in the Lute*   **314**
Composition of Francesco da Milano, (*1497-1543*).
Unpublished Ph.D. diss., University of Iowa. 215p.

FRANCHI, Don Pietro (?-1731)

SARTORI, Claudio. "Franchi, Don Pietro," *MGG* 4:626-27.   **315**

FRANCISQUE, Antoine (1565-1605). *See also:* **129.**

KOCZIRZ, Adolf. "Le Trésor d'Orphée," *ZIMG* 9 (1908):   **316**
251-54.

LESURE, François. "Francisque, Antoine," *MGG* 4:637.   **317**

FUENLLANA, Miguel de (fl. 1550). *See also:* **943, 1253, 1646, 1719.**

ANGLÉS, Higinio. "Dades desconocides sobre Miguel de   **318**
Fuenllana vihuelista," *Revista musical catalana* XXXIII
(1936): 140ff.

319   BOETTICHER, Wolfgang. "Fuenllana, Miguel de," *MGG* 4:1088-91.

320   REIMANN, Hugo. "Das Lautenwerk des Miguel Fuenllana, 1554," *MfM* XXVII (1895):81-91.

FUGGER, Jörg (1517-1569)

321   SCHMID, Ernst F. "Fugger, Jörg," *MGG* 4:1118-26.

FUGGER, Octavianus (1549-1600). *See:* 321.

GALILEI, Vincenzo (1533-1591). *See also:* 1494.

322   CHILESOTTI, Oscar. "Il primo libro di Vincenzo Galilei," *RMI* XV (1908):753-58.

323   ————. "Transcrizioni da un codice musicale di Vincenzo Galilei," in *Atti del Congresso Internazionale di scienze storiche* VIII 1903 (1905):135ff.

324   PALISCA, Claude V. "Galilei, Vincenzo," *MGG* 4:1266-70.

325   ————. "Vincenzo Galilei's Arrangements for Voice and Lute," *Festschrift PLAMENAC*, pp. 207-32.

GALLOT (Family) (fl. seventeenth century)

326   RADKE, Hans. "Bemerkungen zur Lautenisten-Familie Gallot," *Mf* XIII (1960):51-55.

GALLOT D'ANGERS. *See:* 1440.

GALLOT, Jacques (fl. 1670). *See also:* 1459, 1514.

327   BOETTICHER, Wolfgang. "Gallot, Jacques," *MGG* 4:1328-29.

328   CALLAHAN, Claire M. *Jacques Gallot's Pièces de Luth.* Unpublished Master's thesis, Ohio State University, 1963. 244p.

GARSI DA PARMA, Santino (d. 1604)

329   OSTHOFF, Helmuth. *Der Lautenist Santino Garsi da Parma.* Ph.D. diss., published Leipzig: Breitkopf und Härtel, 1926.

44

————. "Garsi da Parma, Santino," *MGG* 4:1398-99. 330

GASTOLDI, Giovanni Giacomo (1556-1622)

ARNOLD, Denis. "Gastoldi, Giovanni G," *MGG* 4:1437-41. 331

GAULTIER, Denis (1600-ca. 1670). *See also:* 328: pp. 84-89, 1514.

FLEISCHER, Oskar. "Denis Gaultier," *VfMw* II (1886): 1-180. 332

HÄFNER, Wolf E. *Die Lautenstücke des Denis Gaultier.* 333
Unpublished Ph.D. diss., Freiburg, 1939.

PETSCHAUER, Roy. "Denis Gaultier and the Unmeasured 334
Prelude," *GR* 36 (1972): 12-15.

REIMANN, Margarite. "Gaultier, Denis," *MGG* 4:471-1477. 335

SHARP, G. B. "Gaultier and Chambonnieres. Two French 336
Tercentenaries," *MT* 113 no. 1558 (1972), pp. 1, 178-81.

GAULTIER, Ennemond (1575-1651)

BOETTICHER, Wolfgang. "Gaultier, Ennemond," *MGG* 337
4:1477-80.

RADKE, Hans. "Bemerkungen zu Lautenisten Ennemond, 338
Jacques und Pierre Gaultier," *ÖMz* XVII (1962): 482-84.

TESSIER, André. "Ennemond Gaultier, Sieur de Neves," 339
Festschrift LAURENCIE, pp. 97-106.

GAULTIER, Jacques (1600-ca. 1660). *See also:* 112, 338, 1151.

LA LAURENCIE, Lionel de. "Le luthiste Jacques Gaultier," 340
RM V/3 (1924): 32-39.

GAULTIER, Pierre (fl. 1638). *See also:* 338, 1192: pp. 106-109.

LAUNAY, Denise. "Gaultier, Pierre," *MGG* 4:1486-87. 341

GEERTSON, Jan van (fl. 1656)

SMIJERS, Albert. "Geertson, Jan van," *MGG* 4:1532-33. 342

GEHEMA, Virginia R. von, Lute-Book, ca. 1640. *See:* **1439.**

GEMINIANI, Francesco Saverio (1680-1762)

343   GIEGLING, Franz. "Geminiani, Francesco S.," *MGG* 4:690-1696.

GERLE, Hans (1500-1571). *See also:* **535.**

344   BOETTICHER, Wolfgang. "Gerle, Hans," *MGG* 4:1804-1807.

345   EITNER, Robert. "Hans Gerle's Lautenbuch von 1532," *MfM* (1871), pp. 211-12.

346   ————. "Hans Gerle's Lautenbuch von 1546 und 1552," *MfM* (1872), p. 38.

347   KIEFHABER, J. S. "Bibliographische Nachrichten von Hans Gerle, dem ältern, berühmten Lautenisten zu Nürnberg im 16. Jahrhundert," *AmZ* XVIII (1918): 309-15, 324-29.

348   PIERCE, Jane. *Hans Gerle: Sixteenth Century Lutenist and Pedagogue.* Unpublished Ph.D. diss., University of North Carolina, Chapel Hill, 1973. 2 vols. (696p.).

349   ————. "Hans Gerle: Sixteenth-Century Lutenist and Pedagogue," *JLSA* VI (1973): 17-29.

350   TAPPERT, Wilhelm. "Die Lautenbücher des Hans Gerle," *MfM* V (1886): 101-11.

GESUALDO, Carlo (1560-1613)

351   JORDAN, Bart. "The Legacy of Carlo Gesualdo, Virtuoso Lutenist-Composer," *GR* 29 (1966): 15-17.

GHIZZOLO, Giovanni (d. 1625)

352   TAGLIAVINI, Luigi F. "Ghizzolo, Giovanni," *MGG* 5:73-75.

GIARDINI, Felice (1716-1796)

353   CUDDLEWORTH, Charles. "Giardini, Felice," *MGG* 5:84-88.

GILLIER, Jean Claude (1667-1737)

BRIQUET, Marie. "Gillier, Jean Claude," *MGG* 5:126-32.   354

GINTZLER, Simon (1512-1578)

BOETTICHER, Wolfgang. "Gintzler, Simon," *MGG* 5:141-42.   355

GIOVANNI Maria da Crema (fl. 1546). *See also:* Toombs, Stephen. *The Lute Ricecares of Giovanni Maria da Crema: A Critical Edition.* Unpublished Master's thesis, University of Washington, 1975.

DARDO, Gianluigi. "Considerazioni sull'opera di Giovan Maria   356
da Crema luitista del Cinquecento," *Collectanea Historiae Musicae* 4 (1966):61-79.

————. "Contributo alla storia del liuto en Italia: Johannes   357
Maria Alemanus e Giovanni Maria da Crema," *Quaderni della Rassegna Musicale* 3 (1965): 143-57.

SLIM. H. Colin. "Gian and Gian Maria, Some Fifteenth- and   358
Sixteenth-Century Namesakes," *MQ* LVII (1971):563-74.

GORLIER, Simon (fl. 1551). *See also:* 925.

LESURE, François. "Gorlier, Simon," *MGG* 5:533-34.   359

GORZANIS, Giacomo (fl. 1564). *See also:* 1516.

BOETTICHER, Wolfgang. "Gorzanis, Giacomo," *MGG*   360
5:534-36.

CHILESOTTI, Oscar. "Jacomo Gorzanis, liutista del   361
Cinquecento," *RMI* XXI (1914): 86-96.

HALBIG, H. "Ein Handschriftliche Lautentabulatur des   362
Giacomo Gorzanis," *Festschrift KROYER*, pp. 102-17.

RADOLE, Giuseppe. "Giacomo Gorzanis 'Leutonista et   363
Cittadena della magnifica città di Trieste'," *KONGRESS 1956*, pp. 525-30.

REICHERT, Georg. "Giacomo Gorzanis Intabolatura di Liuto   364
(1567) als Dur- und Molltonarten-Zyklus," *Festschrift FELLERER*, pp. 428-38.

TONAZZI, Bruno. "Il Cinquecentista Giacomo Gorzanis liutista   365
e cittadino de trieste," *IFr* I (April, 1973):6-21.

GRANATA, Giovanni Battista (fl. 1650). *See also:* 280.

366   SARTORI, Claudio. "Granata, Giovanni Battista," *MGG* 5:681.

GRANDI, Alessandro (d. 1630)

367   ARNOLD, Denis. "Grandi, Alessandro," *MGG* 5:685-89.

GREAVES, Thomas (fl. 1600)

368   FORTUNE, Nigel. "Greaves, Thomas," *MGG* 5:752-53.

GREGORI, Annibale (fl. 1635)

369   TAGLIAVINI, Liugi F. "Gregori, Annibale," *MGG* 5:783-84.

GREGORI, Giovanni Lorenzo (1663-1743)

370   GIEGLING, Franz. "Gregori, Giovanni L.," *MGG* 5:784-85.

GREMBOSZEWSKI, Marcim (1600-1655)

371   KMICIC-MIELESZYNSKI, Wacław. "Charakterystyka tworczosci Marcini Gremboszewskiego, kompozytora gdanskiego," [The Characteristics of the Work of Marcim Gremboszewski, ...] *Zeszyty Naukowe. Panstwowa Wyzsc Szkoła Muzyczna A Gdańsku* XI (1972): 27-62.

GRENERIN, Henri (fl. 1668). *See:* 140

GUERAU, Francesco (d. ca. 1700). *See also:* 840.

372   FORTUNE, Nigel. "Guerau, Francesco," *MGG* 5:1026-27.

HAINHOFER, Philipp

373   TAPPERT, Wilhelm. "Philipp Hainhofer's Lautenbücher, 1603," *MfM* XVII (1885): 29-34.

HALES, Robert (fl. 1600)

374   POULTON, Diana. "The Favorite Singer of Queen Elizabeth I," *Consort* 14 (1957): 24-27.

HALLWIL (Family). *See also:* 1349: pp. 29-33.

FLOTZINGER, Rudolf. "Ein unbekanntes Lautenbuch eines   **375**
Herrn von Hallwil," *Heimatskunde aus dem Seital* (1963-1965).

HÄNDEL, Georg Friedrich (1685-1759)

NIELSEN, Niels K. "Händel's Organ Concertos Reconsidered,"   **376**
[incl. Op. 4 No. 6 Harp-Lute Concerto] *Dansk Aarbog for
Musik Forskning* (1963), p. 10.

HANDFORD, George (fl. 1619)

DOUGHTIE, E. "The Handford Book of Lute Songs [1609],"   **377**
Forum IX (Houston, 1971): 79-80.

HASSE, Johann Adolph (1699-1783). *See:* 1537.

HAYDN, Joseph (1732-1809)

NEEMANN, Hans. "Haydn und die Laute," *Musik im Haus*   **378**
VI/3 (1926).

HEBREO, Giovanni Maria. *See:* 358.

HECKEL, Wolff (1515- ?). *See also:* 539.

BOETTICHER, Wolfgang. "Heckel, Wolff," *MGG* 6:14-16.   **379**

HEINICHEN, Johann David (1683-1729)

HAUSSWALD, Gunter. "Heinichen, Johann David," *MGG*   **380**
6:46-53.

HENESTROSA, Luis Venegas

ANGLÉS, Higinio. ". . . *La musica en la corte de Carlos V, con la*   **381**
*transcription de 'Libro de cifra nueva para tecla, harpa y
vihuela' de Luis Venegas de Henestrosa (1557)."* Barcelona:
C. S. I. S., 1944. 205 + 217p.

MOLL ROQUETA, J. "Musicos en la corte del Cardenal J. Tarera: **382**
L. Venegas de Henestrosa," *AnM* VI (1951): 155-78.

383   WARD, John. "The Editorial Methods of Venegas de Henestrosa," *MD* VI (1952): 105-15.

HOFHAIMER, Paul

384   NOWAK, Leopold. " 'Nach Willen Dein' in den Lautentabulaturen des 16. Jahrhunderts," *Festschrift KOCZIRZ*, pp. 25-29.

HOLBORNE, Anthony (d. 1602?). *See also:* 1019, 1458.

385   BOETTICHER, Wolfgang. "Holborne, Anthony," *MGG* 6:611-13.

386   FLOOD, Gratton. "Anthony Holborne, New Light on Late Tudor Composers," *MT* 69 (1928): 511-12.

387   JEFFERY, Brian. "Anthony Holborne," *MD* XXII (1968): 129-205.

388   ─────. *The Life and Music of Anthony Holborne.* Unpublished Litt. B., Oxford University, 1965.

389   ─────. "The Lute Music of Holborne," *PRMA* 93 (1966-1967): 25-31.

390   KANAZAWA, Masakata. *A. Holborne: An Elizabethan Composer of Instrumental Music.* Unpublished Ph.D. diss., Harvard University, 1961.

HOTMAN (Hautman), Nicolas (d. 1663)

391   BOULAY, Laurence. "Hotman, Nicolas," *MGG* 6:782-83.

392   MOUREAU, François. "Nicolas Hotman, bourgeois de Paris et musicien," *Recherche sur la musique français classique* 13 (1973): 5-22.

HOVE, Joachim van den. *See:* van den Hove, Joachim.

HUME, Tobias (d. 1645)

393   FORTUNE, Nigel. "Hume, Tobias," *MGG* 6:918-19.

HUNT, Arabella (d. 1705)

394   HUSK, William H. "Hunt, Arabella," *Grove* 4:413.

HUREL, Charles (d. 1682). *See also:* 1414.

LAUNAY, Denise. "Hurel, Charles," *MGG* 6:970.   395

HUYGENS, Constantin (1596-1687). *See:* 1669.

JELINEK, Peter Ivan. *See also:* 273.

VOGL, Emil. "Der Lautenist P. Ivan Jelinek, Das Ende der   396
böhmischen Lautenkunst," *Mf* XXII/1 (January-March,
1969): 53-56.

————. "Pater Ivan Jelinek," *Hudebni Věda* 4/4 (1967): 693-96.   397

JOAN Maria da Crema. *See:* Giovanni Maria da Crema.

JOBIN, Bernard (fl. 1570)

INGLEFIELD, R. *A Transcription and Study of Bernard Jobin's*   398
Lute Books of 1572 and 1573. Unpublished Ph.D. diss.,
University of Cincinnati, 1973.

INGLEFIELD, Ruth K. "The Bernhard Jobin Lutebooks,   399
(1572-1573)," *JLSA* VIII (1975): 5-21.

PETER-DE VALLIER, O. "Die Musik in J. Fischarts Dictungen,"   400
AfMw XVIII (1961): 204-22.

JOHNSON, John (d. 1598)

HUMPHRIES, Charles. "Johnson, John,' *MGG* 7:130-31.   401

JOHNSON, Robert (1569?-1633)

BOETTICHER, Wolfgang and David LUMSDEN. "Johnson,   402
Robert," *MGG* 7:133-35.

CUTTS, John P. *The Contribution of Robert Johnson, King's*   403
Musician to Court and Theatrical Entertainments, and the
Tradition of Such Service Prior to 1642. Unpublished Ph.D.
diss., University of Reading (England), 1955.

————. "Robert Johnson: King's Musician in His Majesty's   404
Public Entertainment," *M&L* 36/2 (1955): 110-25.

405   JEFFERY, Brian. "The Lute Music of Robert Johnson," *EM* II
       (1974):105-109.

406   NAGEL, Wilibald. "Annalen der englischen Hofmusik von der Zeit
       Heinrichs VIII bis zum Tode Karl I (1509-1649)," Bielage *MfM*
       26 (1894):40-42.

JONES, Robert (1577-   ?). *See also:* 117, 1169; Adams, Joseph Q. "A
New Song by Robert Jones," *Modern Language Quarterly* I (1940):45-48.

407   CUTTS, John P. "A Reconsideration of the Willow Song," *JAMS*
       X (1957):14-24.

408   FELLOWES, Edmund H. "The Texts of the Song-Books of Robert
       Jones," *M&L* VIII (1927):25-37.

409   FORTUNE, Nigel. "Jones, Robert," *MGG* 7:162-64.

410   PATTISON, K. *An Analysis of the Ayres of Robert Jones.*
       Unpublished M.F.A., University of Georgia, 1965. 86p.

JUDENKÜNIG, Hans (1450-1526). *See also:* 539, 1433.

411   BOETTICHER, Wolfgang. "Judenkünig, Hans," *MGG* 7:223-24.

412   CHIESA, Ruggero. "Storia della letteratura del liuto e della chitarra
       (Hans Judenkünig)," *IFr* III/12 (July, 1975):15-18, III/13
       (October, 1975):15-18.

413   EITNER, Robert. "Hans Judenkünig," *Allgemeine Deutsche
       Biographie* XIV (1881).

414   KOCZIRZ, Adolf. *Der Lautenist Hans Judenkünig.* Unpublished
       Ph.D. diss., Wien, 1903.

415   ————. "Der Lautenist Hans Judenkünig," *SIMG* VI (1904-
       1905:237-314.

KAPSBERGER, Johann (ca. 1575-ca. 1650)

416   BOETTICHER, Wolfgang and Franz GIEGLING. "Kapsberger,
       Johann," *MGG* 7:674-76.

KARGEL, Sixtus (fl. 1570's)

417   BOETTICHER, Wolfgang. "Kargel, Sixtus," *MGG* 7:688-90.

52

EITNER, Robert. "Sixt Kargel," *Allgemeine Deutsche Biographie*   **418**
XV (1882).

KELLER, Gottfried (d. 1721)

TILMOUTH, Michael. "Keller, Gottfried," *MGG* 7:806-808.   **419**

KELLNER, David (1670-1748)

HASSE, Hans. "Kellner, David," *MGG* 7:817-19.   **420**

WIENANDT, Elwyn. "David Kellner's Lautenstücke," *JAMS*   **421**
X (1957): 29-38.

KOHAUT, Joseph (1736-1780)

QWARKA, Rudolf. "Kohaut, Joseph," *MGG* 7:1396-97.   **422**

KREBS, Johann Ludwig (1713-1780). *See also:* Horstman, Jean. *The Instrumental Music of J. L. Krebs.* Unpublished Ph.D. diss., Boston University, 1959. 314p. UM 59-03465.

LÖFFLER, H. "Johann Ludwig Krebs, . . . sein Leben und   **423**
Werken," *Bach Jahrbuch* (1930), pp. 100-129.

TITTEL, Karl. "Krebs, Johann L.," *MGG* 7:1726-36.   **424**

KREMBERG, Jacob (1650-1716). *See also:* 970.

BOETTICHER, Wolfgang. "Kremberg, Jacob," *MGG* 7:1748-50.   **425**

KOCZIRZ, Adolf. "J. Kremberg. Musikalische Gemüths-   **426**
Ergötzung oder Arien," *Die Gitarre* III (1921-1922):35ff.

KÜHNEL, August (b. 1645?)

PAULS, Karl. "Kühnel, August," *MGG* 7:1857-58.   **427**

LA BARRE, Joseph (1633-1678)

WALLON, Simon. "La Barre, Joseph," *MGG* 8:4-5.   **428**

LA BARRE, Pierre (1572-1628)

429   WALLON, Simon. "La Barre, Pierre," *MGG* 8:5-6.

LAGARDE, Pierre de (1717-1792)

430   BRIQUET, Marie. "Lagarde, Pierre," *MGG* 8:69-70.

LA GROTE, Nicolas de (ca. 1530-ca. 1600). *See also:* 1419.

431   LEBÈGUE, R. "Ronsard corrigé par un de ses musiciens," *RMl* (July, 1957), pp. 71-72.

432   LESURE, François. "La Grotte, Nicolas de," *MGG* 8:74-75.

LANDI, Stefano (ca. 1590-1655)

433   ABERT, Anna A. "Landi, Stefano," *MGG* 8:162-63.

LANIER, Nicholas (1588-1666). *See:* 1144, 1482.

LASSUS, Roland de

434   BOETTICHER, Wolfgang. "Les Oeuvres de Roland de Lassus mises en Tablature," in *Le Luth et sa musique.* Edited by J. Jacquot. Paris: CNRS, 1958, pp. 143-54.

LA TOUR, Alexander de. *See:* 1183.

LAWES, Henry (1595-1662). *See also:* 1151, 1702.

435   DUCKLES, Vincent. "Lawes, Henry," *MGG* 8:392-95.

436   EVANS, W. M. Henry Lawes, *Musician and Friend of Poets.* New York: Modern Language Association, 1941.

437   HART, E. Ford. "Introduction to Henry Lawes," *M&L* XXXII (1951): 217-25, 328-41.

LAWES, William (1602-1645)

438   CUTTS, John P. "British Museum Additional MS. 31432 William Lawes' Writing for the Theater and the Court," *The Library* 5th ser. VII (1952): 225-34.

HART, E. Ford. "Caroline Lyrics and Contemporary Song-Books," **439**
The Library 5th ser. VIII (1953): 89-110.

LEFKOWITZ, Murry. *William Lawes.* London: Routledge & Kegan **440**
Paul, 1959.

LEIGHTON, William (d. 1616). *See also:* **1021, 1023.**

HURAY, Peter G. le. "Leighton, William," *MGG* 8:539-40. **441**

LE MAIRE, Jean. *See:* **1521.**

LE ROY, Adrian (1520-1589). *See also:* **7, 17.**

LESURE, François. "Le Roy, Adrian," *MGG* 8:660-62. **442**

MORCOURT, Richard de. "Adrian Le Roy et le psaumes pour **443**
luth," *AnnMl* III (1955): 179-212.

LE SAGE DE RICHÉE, Philip Franz (fl. 1695)

EITNER, Robert. "Ein wenig bekanntes Lautenwerk Cabinet **444**
der Lauten (1695)," *MfM* XXI/1 (1889): 9-24.

WORTMANN, Toni. *Philipp Franz le Sage de Richée und sein* **445**
Cabinet der Lauten. Unpublished Ph.D., Wien, 1919.

LESPINE, Charles (fl. 1619)

LACHEVRE, F. *Un jouer de luth et compositeur des cours* **446**
pricipières. Autheur dramatique et poete Charles Lespine
Parisien . . . . Paris: Giraud-Baden, 1935. 216p.

LOBKOWITZ, August (Philip) Hyazinth (1680-1735)

SCHAAL, Richard. "Lobkowitz, August H.," *MGG* 8:1069-72. **447**

LOSY (Logi) VON LOSINTHAL, Graf Anton (1650-1721). *See also:* **273.**

BOETTICHER, Wolfgang. "Losy von Losinthal, Graf Anton," **448**
MGG 8:1219-21.

VOGL, Emil. "Zur Biographie Losy's (von Losinthal)," *Mf* **449**
XIV (1961): 189-92.

LOWTHER, Christopher (fl. 1637)

450 BEECHEY, G. "Christopher Lowther's Lute-Book," *GSJ* XXIV (1971): 51-59.

MACE, Denis (fl. 1643)

451 JACQUOT, Jean. "Mace, Denis," *MGG* 8:1381-83.

MACE, Thomas (1623-1709)

452 GILL, Donald. "The Lute and Musick's Monument," *GSJ* III (1950): 9-11.

453 JACQUOT, Jean. "Musick's Monument de Thomas Mace (1676) et l'evolution de goût musicale en Angleterre," *RMl* XXXIV (1952): 21-37.

454 MACKERNESS, E. D. "T. Mace: Additions to a Biography," *MMR* (1953), pp. 43-46.

455 ―――. "Thomas Mace and the Fact of Reasonableness," *MMR* (1955), pp. 211-13, 235-39.

456 THACKERAY, R. M. "Thomas Mace," *MT* (1951), pp. 306-307.

457 WATSON, H. "Thomas Mace, the Man, the Book, the Instrument," *PRMA* (1908), pp. 87-109.

MAGDALENE, Mary

458 HEARTZ, Daniel. "Mary Magdalene, Lutenist," *JLSA* V (1972): 52-67.

MAJER, Joseph F. B. C. (1689-1768)

459 REICHERT, Georg. "Majer, Joseph," *MGG* 8:1531-32.

MALETTY, Jehan de

460 THIBAULT, G. "Les Amours de P. de Ronsard mises en musique par Jehan de Maletty (1578)," *Festschrift LAURENCIE*, pp. 61-72.

MARINONI, Girolomo (d. 1647)

ARNOLD, Denis. "Marinoni, Girolomo," *MGG* 8:1657.   **461**

MARTIN, François (fl. 1663). *See:* **100**.

MARTIN, Philipp (Martino, Filippo) (fl. 1730)

NEEMANN, Hans. "Philipp Martin, ein vergessener Lautenist,"   **462**
ZfMw (1926), pp. 545-65.

MASON, Mathias (fl. 1580-1609). *See:* **1144**.

MATELART, Joanne(s) (fl. 1559)

CHILESOTTI, Oscar. "Joanne Matelart, Fiamengo Musico,"   **463**
Gazetta Musicale di Milano 40 (1885):4ff.

SPIESSENS, Godelieve. "Matelart, Joannes," *MGG* 8:1783-85.   **464**

MATHEW, Richard (fl. 1652)

HAYES, Gerald. "Music in the Boteler Muniments," *GSJ*   **465**
8 (1955):43-46.

SIMPSON, Adrienne. "Richard Mathew and The Lute's Apology,"   **466**
LSJ 8 (1966):41ff.

————. *A Study of Richard Mathew's 'The Lute's Apology for*   **467**
her Excellency' (1654). Unpublished Master's thesis, King's
College, London, 1966.

MATTEIS, Nicola (fl. 1670's). *See also:* **1017**.

EVANS, Peter A. "Matteis, Nicola," *MGG* 8:1792-93.   **468**

McCREADE, Andrew D. "Nicola Matteis-English Composer at   **469**
the Hapsburg Court," *M&L* 48 (1968):127-37.

NETTL, P. "An English Musician at the Court of Charles VI   **470**
in Vienna," *MQ* 28 (1942):318-28.

MAYNARD, John (1577- after 1622)

HARWOOD, Ian. "John Maynard and 'The XII Wonders of the   **471**
World'," *LSJ* IV (1962):7-16.

472   ———. "Maynard, John," *MGG* 8:1840-41.

473   TRAFICANTE, Frank. "Music for the Lyra Viol: The Printed Sources," *LSJ* VIII (1966): 7-24.

MEDICI, Giulio

474   SCHAAL, Richard. "Medici, Giulio," *MGG* 8:1889-92.

MEDICIS, Johannis Maria de. *See:* **358.**

MELLI (Megli) Domenico (fl. 1550's)

475   FORTUNE, Nigel. "Melli (Megli) Domenico," *MGG* 9:17-18.

MELLI, Pietro (fl. 1615)

476   DART, Thurston. "Melli, Pietro," *Grove* 5:663.

MERTEL, Elias (fl. 1613)

477   DORFMÜLLER, Kurt. "Mertel, Elias," *MGG* 9:136-37.

MERULO, Claudio (1533-1604)

478   CHILESOTTI, Oscar. "Claudio Merulo nelle intavolatura di liuto," *Numero Unico Claudio Merulo* (Parma, June, 1904).

MEZANGEAU, René (d. 1638). *See also:* **126.**

479   LE MOEL, M. "Pour meillure biographie de Mezangeau," *Recherches sur la musique française classique* III (1963): 21-23.

480   ROLLIN, Monique. "Mezangeau, René," *MGG* 9:261.

MILAN, Luis (1500-1560)

481   JACOBS, Charles (ed.). *Luis de Milan-El Maestro.* University Park, Pennsylvania: Pennsylvania State University Press, 1971, pp. 1-27, 295-319.

482   ROMEU I FIGUERAS, J. "Literatura Valencia en El Cortesano de Luis Milan," *Rivista Valenciana de Filologia* I (1951): 313-39.

SCHRADE, Leo. "Luys Milan, the Vihuelista," *GR* IX (1949): 19-21. **483**

TREND, J. B. *Luis Milan and the Vihuelistas.* New York: Hispanic Society of America, 1925. **484**

VAN DEN MEER, J. H. "Het 'Libro de musica de Vehuelo [*sic*] de mano' van Luys Milan," *Mens en Melody* 14 (1959):281-87. **485**

WARD, John. "Milan, Don Luis," *MGG* 9:289-92. **486**

MILANUZI, Carlo (d. 1647)

TAGLIAVINI, Luigi. "Milanuzi, Carlo," *MGG* 9:292-93. **487**

MILIONI, Pietro (fl. 1620's)

TAGLIAVINI, Luigi. "Milioni, Pietro," *MGG* 9:304. **488**

MILLERAN, René (d. after 1690)

ROLLIN, Monique. "Milleran, René," *MGG* 9:336. **489**

MINGUET Y YROL, Pablo (d. 1801)

QUEROL, Miguel. "Minguet Y Yrol, Pablo," *MGG* 9:350-51. **490**

MOLINARO, Simone (1565-1615)

SARTORI, Claudio. "Molinaro, Simone," *MGG* 9:434-35. **491**

DART, Thurston. "Simone Molinaro's Lute Book of 1599," *M&L* 27 (1947):258-61. **492**

RONCAGLIA, G. "Simone Molinaro," *RMI* XIX (1941):184-86. **493**

MOLITOR, Simon (1766-1848)

ZUTH, Josef. *Simon Molitor und die Wiener Gitarristik (um 1800).* Unpublished Ph.D. diss., Wien, 1920. **494**

MONTBUYSON, Victor de (fl. 1610)

495   ARNHEIM, A. "Livre de tablature de luth pour Madame, Elisabet, Princess de Hessen commencá par Victor de Montbuyson 6 dernier Janvier 1611," *SIMG* X (1908):412ff.

MONTESARDO, Girolamo (d. after 1620)

496   PAOLUCCI, R. "La Cappella Musicale del Duomo di Fano," *Note d'Archivo* III (1926):100-101.

497   TAGLIAVINI, Luigi F. "Montesardo, Girolamo," *MGG* 9:509-10.

MORITZ, Landgraf von Hessen (1572-1662)

498   ENGLEBRECHT, Christine. "Moritz, Landgraf von Hessen," *MGG* 9:584-86.

MORLAYE, Guilleaume (1515- ?). *See also:* 56, 925.

499   LESURE, François. "Morlaye, Guilleaume," *MGG* 9:588-89.

500   PIDOUX, Pierre. "Les Psaumes D'Antoine de Mornable, Guillaume Morlaye et Pierre Certon. (1546, 1554, 1555). Étude Comparative," *AnnMl* V (1957):179-98.

MORLEY, Thomas (1558-1602). *See also:* 222, 1021, 1023, 1487.

501   BECK, Sydney. "The Case of 'O Mistress Mine'," *Renaissance News* VI (1953):19-23.

502   DART, Thurston. "Discussion" [of 'O Mistress Mine'] *Renaissance News* VII (1954):15-17.

503   ———. "Morley's Consort Lessons of 1599," *PRMA* 74 (1947-1948):1-9.

504   DOUGHTIE, Edward. "Robert Southwell and Morley's 'First Booke of Ayres'," *LSJ* IV (1962):28ff.

505   DUCKLES, Vincent. "New Light on 'O Mistress Mine'," *Renaissance News* VII (1954):98-100.

506   GREER, David. "What if a Day"—An Examination of the Words and Music," *M&L* XLIII (1962):304-19.

507   HARMAN, Richard. "Morley, Thomas," *MGG* 9:589-95.

McGRADY, R. J. "Thomas Morley's 'First Booke of Ayres',"   **508**
Music Review 33 (1972): 171-76.

SPENCER, Robert. "Two Missing Lute Parts for Morley's Consort   **509**
Lessons," *LSJ* IV (1962): 28ff.

MOULINIÉ, Etienne (1600- ?). *See also:* **1420.**

BALUFFE, A. "Moliere et Moulinié a Carcassonne en 1652,"   **510**
Le Menestrel IX (1894).

LAUNAY, Denise. "Moulinié, Etienne," *MGG* 9:674-75.   **511**

————. "Notes sur Etienne Moulinié, maître de la musique de   **512**
Gaston d'Orleans," *Festschrift MASSON*, pp. 67-78.

MOUTON, Charles (ca. 1626-ca. 1699?). *See also:* **1514.**

LINDGREN, A. "Ein Lautenbuch von Mouton," *MfM* XXIII   **513**
(1891): 5-15.

ROLLIN, Monique. "La Suite pour luth dans l'oeuvre de Charles   **514**
Mouton," *RM* no. 226 (1955): 76-88.

TESSIER, André. "Le Portrait du luthiste Mouton, par F. De   **515**
Troy au Musée de Louvre," *La Revue de L'Art* (1925): 127ff.

VERCHALY, André. "Mouton, Charles," *MGG* 9:679.   **516**

MUDARRA, Alonso (1520-1580). *See also:* **1519.**

ALATORRE, Margit F. "Sobre los textos poético en Juan   **517**
Vazquez, Mudarra y Narváez," *Nueva Revista de Filologiá
Hispánica* VI (1952): 35-36.

FELLERER, Gustav K. "Josquins Missa 'Faisant Regretz' in der   **518**
Vihuela-transkription von Mudarra und Narváez," *Festschrift
NEUSS*, pp. 179-84.

RICHARDSON, Jerry. [The Fantasias of Mudarra, Books 1   **519**
and 2; title tentative] Master's thesis. San Jose State
University, forthcoming.

WARD, John. "Mudarra, Alonso de," *MGG* 9:843-44.   **520**

————. "The Use of Borrowed Material in 16th-Century   **521**
Instrumental Music," *JAMS* V (1952): 88-98.

MURCIA, Santiago de

522   MACHADO-LOWENFELD, Elena. *Santiago de Murcia's Book of Tablatures for the Spanish Baroque Guitar.* Master's thesis, City College of the City University of New York, forthcoming.

MYLIUS, Johann (1585- ?)

523   GIESBERT, Franz. "Mylius, Johann Daniel," *MGG* 9:1236-37.

NANINO, Giovanni Maria (ca. 1545-1607)

524   d'ALESSI, Giovanni. "Nanino, Giovanni Maria," *MGG* 9:1256-58.

NARVÁEZ, Luis de (1500-1555). *See also:* 517, 518, 1733, 1734.

525   WARD, John. "Narváez, Luis de," *MGG* 9:1268-69.

NAUMANN, Johann Gottlieb (1741-1801)

526   ENGLÄNDER, Richard. "Naumann, Johann G.," *MGG* 9:1288-95.

527   ————. "Zu J. G. Naumanns Duo für Laute und Glas harmonika," *Mf* 11 (1958): 199.

NAUWACH, Johann (1595- ?)

528   EINSTEIN, A. "Ein unbekannter Druck aus der Frühzeit der Monodie," *SIMG* XIII (1912): 288-96.

529   VOLKMANN, H. "Johann Nauwachs Leben," *ZfMw* IV (1922): 553-62.

530   ————. "Johann Nauwach," *Die Musik* XV/12 (1923): 862-65.

NEGRI, Cesare 'detto il Trombone' (1546- ?)

531   KAST, Paul. "Negri, Cesare," *MGG* 9:1359-60.

NERUDA, Jan Jiri (1707-1780)

532   BUŽGA, Jaroslaw. "Neruda, Jan J.," *MGG* 9:1378-79.

NEWSIDLER, Hans (1510-1563). *See also:* 1432.

CHILESOTTI, Oscar. "Di Hans Newsidler e di un'antica   **533**
intavolatura tedesca di liuto," *RMI* I (1894):48-59

DORFMÜLLER, Kurt. "Neusidler, Hans," *MGG* 9:1409-10.   **534**

EITNER, Robert. "Lautenbücher des XVI Jahrhunderts,"   **535**
MfM III (1871):210-21.

————. "Zwei Lautenbücher von 1536 und 1566," *MfM*   **536**
III (1871):152-56.

LINDGREN, A. "En lutbok från 1500-talet," *Svensk*   **537**
Musiktidning II/4 (1882), II/5 (1882).

PÄFFGEN, Peter. *Die Stellung Hans Newsidlers in der*   **538**
Lautenistik des 16. Jahrhunderts. [The position of Hans
Newsidler in 16th-Century German Lute Music.] Ph.D. diss.,
Köln, forthcoming.

PODOLSKI, Michel. "Le Juden Tantz (Analyse et Transcription),"   **539**
[H. Neusidler, H. Judenkünig und Wolff Heckel]. *Belgisch*
Tijdschrift voor Muziekwetenschaft (1963), pp. 29-38.

NEWSIDLER, Konrad (fl. 1564)

DORFMÜLLER, Kurt. "Neusidler, Konrad," *MGG* 9:1408.   **540**

NEWSIDLER, Melchior (1507-1590). *See also:* 536.

DORFMÜLLER, Kurt. "Neusidler, Melchior," *MGG* 9:1407-   **541**
1408.

EITNER, Robert. "Melchior Neusidler," *Allgemeine Deutsche*   **542**
Biographie XXIII (1886).

LAYER, A. "Melchior Neusidler in *Lebensbilder aus dem*   **543**
Bayerischen Schwaben V (1956):180-97.

NIVERS, Guillaume G. (1632-1714?). *See also:* Pruitt, William.

"Bibliographie des Oeuvres de Guillaume G. Nivers," *Recherche*
sur la musique française classique 13 (1973):133-56.

GARROS, Madeleine. "Nivers, Guillaume Gabriel," *MGG*   **544**
9:1539-40.

NOTARI, Angelo (d. 1664)

545   BOORMAN, Stanley. "Notari, Porter and the Lute," *LSJ* XIII (1971): 28-35.

546   SPINK, Ian. "Angelo Notari and his Prime Musiche Nuove," *MMR* LXXXVII (1957): 168-77.

OCHSENKUM, Sebastian (1521-1574)

547   DORFMÜLLER, Kurt. "Ochsenkum, Sebastian," *MGG* 9:1824-25.

548   EITNER, Robert. "Lautenbuch von 1558," *MfM* IV (1872): 52-55.

PADBRUÉ, David Janszoon

549   NOSKE, Frits. "David Janszoon Padbrué, corael-luytslager-vlascoper," [David Janszoon Padbrué, choral singer-lutenist-flax merchant]. *Festschrift LENAERTS*, pp. 197-86.

PALADIN [Paladino], Giovanni Paolo (d. 1566). *See also:* 1465.

550   LESURE, François. "Paladin, Giovanni Paolo," *MGG* 10:651.

551   ———. "G. G. Paladino et son Première livre de luth, 1560," *RMI* (1958): 170-83.

PASCH (Basch), Gottfried? (fl. 1679). *See:* 703.

PAUMANN, Konrad (1415-1473)

552   HENNING, Rudolf and Uta HENNING, (transl.) "German Lute Tablature and Conrad Paumann," *LSJ* XV (1973): 7-10.

553   KRAUTWURST, Franz. "Paumann, Konrad," *MGG* 10:968-71.

PĘKIEL, Bartholomij (d. 1670)

554   FEICHT, Hieronim. "Pękiel, Bartholomij," *MGG* 10:1001-1003.

PELLEGRINI, Domenico (d. after 1650)

555   BELLOW, Alexander. "Domenico Pellegrini," *GR* 29 (1966): 23-24.

556   BOETTICHER, Wolfgang. "Pellegrini, Domenico," *MGG* 10:1008-1009.

PEPUSCH, Johann Christoph (1667-1732)

CUDWORTH, Charles. "Pepusch, Christoph," *MGG* 10:1026-33.   **557**

PERICHON, Jean [Julien Perrichon] (1566-1600). *See also:* 1191.

LESURE, François. "Perrichon, Jean," *MGG* 10:1085-86.   **558**

PERRINE, ——? (d. 1700)

ROLLIN, Monique. "Perrine," *MGG* 10:1089.   **559**

PHALÉSE, Pièrre (1510-1573)

QUITTARD, Henri. "L'Hortus Musarum (P. Phalése) de 1552-   **560**
1553 et les arrangements de pièces polyphoniques pour voix
seule et luth," *SIMG* VIII (1907): 254-75.

ROBYNS-BEQUART, Godelieve. Phalése, Pièrre," *MGG*   **561**
10:1182-83.

————. *"Les Livres de luth de Pièrre Phalése. Étude et*   **562**
transcription de L'Hortus Musarum, 1552-1553."
Unpublished Lizentiatschrift, Katolische Universität, Löwen,
1956.

WOTQUENNE-PLATTEL, Alfred. "Étude sur l'Hortus   **563**
Musarum de Pièrre Phalése," *Revue des Bibliotheques et*
Archives de Belgique I (1903): 48-67.

PHILIPPS, Peter (1560- ?)

STEELE, John. "Philipps, Peter," *MGG* 10:1203-1208.   **564**

PICCININI, Alessandro (1560-1638)

BUETENS, Stanley. "The Instructions of Alessandro Piccinini,"   **565**
JLSA II (1969): 6-17.

KINSKY, Georg. "Alessandro Piccinini und sein Arciliuto,"   **566**
AMl X (1938): 103-18.

TAGLIAVINI, Luigi F. "Piccinini, Alessandro," *MGG*   **567**
10:1235-37.

VATIELLI, F. "L'ultimo liutista," *RMI* 42 (1938): 469-91.   **568**

PICKERING, Jane (fl. 1616). *See also:* 506.

569   KELLY, Thomas. "Notes on the Jane Pickering Lute-Book," *JLSA* I (1968): 19-23.

PIFARO, Marc'Antonio (fl. 1550's)

570   BOETTICHER, Wolfgang. "Pifaro, Marc'Antonio," *MGG* 10:1270.

PILKINGTON, Francis (d. 1638)

571   COXON, Carolyn. "Pilkington, Francis," *MGG* 10:1276-77.

572   NEWTON, Richard, "The Lute Music of Francis Pilkington," *LSJ* I (1959): 31-38.

PINELL, ——? (fl. 1650). *See also:* 100, 140.

573   LESURE, François. "Pinell," *MGG* 10:1282-83.

574   ———. "Abhandlung über Pinell," *RMl* (1955): 186-87.

PISADOR, Diego (1509-1557). *See also:* 1516, 1721.

575   CORTES, N. A. "Diego Pisador: algunos datos biograficos," *Boletin de la Biblioteca Menédez y Pelayo* III (1921): 331-35.

576   HONEGGER, Marc. *Les Messes de Josquin des Pres dans la tablature de Diego Pisador* (*Salamanca 1552*), *Contribution a l'étude des alterations au XVIe siècle.* University of Paris, 1968. 2 vols.

577   ———. "La Tabulature de Diego Pisador et le probleme des alterations au XVIe siècle," *RMl* LIX (1973): 38-59.

578   HUTCHINSON, Loving. *The Vihuela Music of Diego Pisador.* Unpublished Master's thesis, Eastman School of Music, Rochester, 1937.

579   WARD, John. "Pisador, Diego," *MGG* 10:1297-98.

PITONI, Giovanni (fl. 1669). *See:* 44.

PLAYFORD, John (1623-1694). *See also:* Nelson, Russel C. *John Playford and the English Amateur Musician.* (*2 vols. An Edition of Selected Publications of Music*). Unpublished Ph.D. diss., University of Iowa, 1966. 560p. UM 67-02659.

DEAN-SMITH, Margaret. "Playford, John," 10:1344-52.   **580**

POLONOIS (Polonais), Jacob. *See also:* **218;** entry under Reys, Jakob.

OPIENSKI, Henryk. "Jacob le Polonois et Jacobus Reys,"   **581**
Festschrift REIMANN, pp. 349-53.

PORTER, Walter (d. 1659). *See also:* **1151.**

ARKWRIGHT, G. E. P. "An English Pupil of Monteverdi,"   **582**
Musical Antiquary IV (1913): 236-57.

BOORMAN, S. H. *A Critical Study and Partial Transcription*   **583**
of Madrigals and Ayres by William [sic] *Porter, (London,*
1632). Unpublished Master's thesis, London, 1968.

HUGHES, C. W. "Porter, A Pupil of Monteverdi," *MQ* XX   **584**
(1934): 278-88.

SPINK, Ian. "Porter, Walter," *MGG* 10:1478-80.   **585**

————— "Walter Porter and the Last Book of English   **586**
Madrigals," *AMl* XXVI (1954): 18-36.

PORTO, Allegro (ca. 1590-1625?)

KAST, Paul. "Porto, Allegro," *MGG* 10:1483-84.   **587**

RADINO, Giovanni (before 1539-after 1607)

DAMERINI, Adelmo. "Radino, Giovanni," *MGG* 10:1854-55.   **588**

RADOLT, Wenzel Ludwig (1667-1716)

BOETTICHER, Wolfgang. "Radolt, Wenzel Ludwig," *MGG*   **589**
10:1857-58.

RASCHKE, Friedrich Wilhelm (fl. 1670). *See:* **703.**

REICHARDT, Johann

GÜTTLER, H. "Johann Reichardt, ein preussischer Lautenist,"   **590**
KONGRESS 1930, pp. 118-24.

REUSNER, Esaias, Sr. (d. ca. 1669), Jr. (1636-1679). *See also:* 1509: pp. 504-10, 515-20.

591   DORFMÜLLER, Kurt. "Reusner," *MGG* 11:331-33.

592   GURLITT, W. "Ein Beitrag zur Biographie des Lautenisten Esajas Resusner," *SIMG* 14 (1912-1913):49-51, 278.

593   KOCZIRZ, Adolf. "Eine Titleauflage aus dem Jahre 1697 von Esaias Reussners, Erfreuliche Lautenlust," *ZfMw* VIII (1925-1926): 636-40.

594   KOLETSCHKA, Karl. *Esaias Reusner der Jungers und seine Bedeutung für die deutsche Lautenmusik des XVII Jahrhunderts.* Unpublished Ph.D. diss., Wien, 1927.

595   ————. "Esaias Reusner der Jungers und seine Bedeutung für die deutsche Lautenmusik des XVII Jahrhunderts," *StMw* (1929): 3-45.

596   ————. "Esajas Reusner Vater und Sohn und ihre Choral-Bearbeitungen für die Laute," *Festschrift KOCZIRZ*, pp. 14-17.

597   SCHERING, Arnold. "Reusner," *Magazin Leipzigs* II (1926): 101ff., 414-20.

598   SPARMANN, A. *Esajas Reusner und die Lauten-Suite.* Unpublished Ph.D. diss., Berlin, 1926.

599   TAPPERT, Wilhelm. "Esajas Reusner, der Kammerlautenist des Grossen Kurfürsten," *MfM* IX (1900): 135-52.

REYMANN, Matthäus (1565-   ?). *See also:* 206.

600   DORFMÜLLER, Kurt. "Reymann, Matthäus," *MGG* 11:354.

REYS, Jakob (ca. 1545-ca. 1605). *See also:* 581; entry under Polonois, Jacob.

601   FEICHT, Hieronim. "Reys, Jakob," *MGG* 11:354.

RHEDANUS, ————?

602   LAND, J. P. N. "Rhedanus, een Liutenist uit Theden," *Tijdschrift der Vereeniging voor Noord-Nederlands Muziekgeschiedenis* I (1885): 202ff.

RIBAYAZ, Lucas Ruiz de (fl. 1677)

QUEROL, Miguel. "Ruiz de Ribayaz, Lucas," *MGG* 11:1089. **603**

STRIZICH, Robert. "A Spanish Guitar Tutor: Ruiz de Ribayaz's **604**
Luz y Norte Musical (1677)," *JLSA* VII (1974): 51-81.

RICHARD (Family)

DUFOURCQ, Norbert. "Notes sur les Richard, Musiciens **605**
Français du XVIIe siècle," *RMl* XXXVI (1954): 116-33.

RIGAUD, Louys de (fl. 1623)

VERCHALY, André. "Rigaud, Louys de," *MGG* 11:504. **606**

ROBINSON, Thomas (d. 1610). *See also:* **506.**

AUSTIN, David L. *Thomas Robinson's 'The Schoole of Musicke.'* **607**
Unpublished Master's thesis, University of Michigan, 1967.

BURLESON, Richard F. *Thomas Robinson's Schoole of Musicke:* **608**
a Lute Tutor of 1603. Unpublished Master's thesis, University
of Washington, 1967.

HARMAN, Richard. "Robinson, Thomas," *MGG* 11:584-85. **609**

KINKELDEY, Otto. "Thomas Robinson's 'Schoole of Musicke'," **610**
BAMS 1 (1936): 7.

ROMANIN, Carlo. *See:* **44.**

RONSARD, Pierre de (1524-1585)

PHOTIADES, Constantin. *Ronsard et son Luth.* Paris, 1925. **611**

RONTANI, Raffaello (d. 1622)

FORTUNE, Nigel. "Rontani, Raffaello," *MGG* 11:890-91. **612**

―――. "A Handlist of Printed Italian Secular Monody Books **613**
1602-1635," *RMA* III (1963).

ROSSI, Salome (ca. 1570-1630)

614   NEWMAN, Joel. *The Madrigals of Solomone Rossi.* Unpublished
Ph.D. diss., Columbia University, 1962.

ROSSETER, Philipp (1568-1623)

615   FORTUNE, Nigel. "Rosseter, Philipp," *MGG* 11:930-32.

616   ————. "Philip Rosseter and His Songs." *LSJ* VII (1965): 7-14.

617   HARWOOD, Ian. "Rosseter's 'Lessons for Consort' of 1609," *LSJ*
VIII (1965): 15-23.

618   VLAM, Christian and Thurston DART. "Rosseters in Holland,"
GSJ XI (1958): 63-69.

ROTTA, Antonio (1496-1548)

619   MALACEK, A. R. "Anton Rotta, eine biographische Skizze,"
Festschrift KOCZIRZ, pp. 20-23.

620   ————. *Der Paduaner Lautenmeister Antonio Rotta, ca. 1495-
1548.* Unpublished Ph.D. diss., Wien, 1930.

621   RADKE, Hans. "Rotta, Antonio," *MGG* 11:995-96.

RUDE, Johannes (1555-1601?). *See also:* 206.

622   DORFMÜLLER, Kurt. "Rude, Johannes," *MGG* 11:1057-58.

623   LOBAUGH, H. Bruce. "Johann Rude's Flores Musicae (1600),"
LSJ XIV (1972): 5-12.

RUGGIERI, Giovanni Maria (d. after 1720)

624   CHIESA, Mary. "Ruggieri, Giovanni Maria," *MGG* 11:1085-86.

SABBATINI, Pietro Paolo (ca. 1600-after 1657)

625   KAST, Paul. "Sabbatini, Pietro Paolo," *MGG* 11:1216-18.

SALÈPICO, Josquino

626   SAMARELLI, Francesco. "Josquino Salèpico vel Salèm da
Malfetta, liutista e musicista del secolo XVI," *Note d'Archivo*
IX (1932): 130-40.

SAINT-LUC, Jacques de (1616-after 1700)

ROLLIN, Monique. "Saint-Luc, Jacques de," *MGG* 11:1262.   627

VAN DER STRAETEN, Edmund. *Jacques de Saint Luc Luthiste*   628
Athois du XVII Siècle. Paris: Maison Schott, 1887.

SAN MARTINI, Pietro (1636-1700). *See also:* 1110.

FABBRI, Mario. "San Martini, Pietro," *MGG* 11:1372-73.   629

SANTA MARIA, Tomas de (d. 1570)

KASTNER, Santiago. "Santa Maria, Tomas de," *MGG*   630
11:1378-79.

SANZ, Gaspar (1640-1710)

KOCZIRZ, Adolf. "Gaspar Sanz' Unterweisung in der Musik der   631
Spanischen Gitarre (1674)," *Die Gitarre* I (1919-1920):120ff.

MANNS, Jerrold. *Gaspar Sanz. "Instrucción de Música Sobre*   632
la Guitarra"-Translation and Commentary. Master's thesis,
Case Western Reserve University, forthcoming.

ROLLIN, Monique. "Sanz, Gaspar," *MGG* 11:1387-88.   633

ZAYAS, Rodrigo de. "Gaspar Sanz," *Consort* 31 (1975):132-41.   634

————. "Gaspar Sanz and His Music," *GR* 40 (1970):2-32.   635
[Includes transcription of Book I.]

SARACINI, Claudio (1586-1650)

SZABOLCSI, Bence. "Saracini, Claudio," *MGG* 11:1379-99.   636

SCHEIDLER, Christian Gottlieb (1752-1815)

ZUTH, Josef. "Über Christian Gottlieb Scheidler,"   637
Festschrift KOCZIRZ, pp. 50-56.

SCHLICK, Arnold (1460?-1521?)

EITNER, Robert. "Arnold Schlick's Tabulaturen etlicher   638
Lobgesang auff die Orgeln und Lauten von 1512," *MfM* I
(1869):115-27.

639   KATTERBA, Karin. "Schlick, Arnolt," *MGG* 11:1817-20.

SCHMALL VON LEBENDORF, Nicolas (1592-   ?)

640   KLIMA, Josef. "Die Tanze des Nicolas Schmall von Lebendorf (1613)," *ÖMZ* 21 (1966):460-61.

SECKENDORF, Karl Sigmund (fl. 1750)

641   HÄRTWIG, Dieter. "Seckendorf, Karl Sigmund," *MGG* 12:451-52.

SEVERI, F. (d. 1630)

642   MISCHIATI, Oscar. "Severi, F.," *MGG* 12:596-97.

SEVERINO, Giulio (d. after 1601)

643   ROLLIN, Monique. "Severino, Giulio," *MGG* 12:598.

SPINACINO, Francesco (d. after 1507). *See also:* **1666, 1700.**

644   DISERTORI, Benvenuto and Hans RADKE. "Spinacino, Francesco," *MGG* 12:1046-47.

645   NORDSTROM, Lyle E. *An Examination of the First Book of Lute Tablatures by Francesco Spinacino.* D.M.A project, Stanford University, 1969. 69p

STEFANI, Giovanni (fl. 1623)

646   TAGLIAVINI, Luigi F. "Stefani, Giovanni," *MGG* 12:1203-1204.

STOBÄUS, Johann (1580-1646)

647   HÄRTWIG, Dieter. "Stobäus, Johann," *MGG* 12:1362-65.

STRAUBE, Rudolf (1717?-1785)

648   RADKE, Hans. "Straube, Rudolf," *MGG* 12:1445-46.

STROBEL, Valentin, Sr. (1580-1640), Jr. (1611-1669)

72

RADKE, Hans. "Strobel de Strasbourg, Valentin," *MGG*   **649**
12:1610-11.

STUART, John (fl. 1615)

CARMACK, Murry. *The So-Called John Stuart Lute Book.*   **650**
Unpublished Master's thesis, Harvard University, 1967.

SWEELINCK, Jan Pieterszoon (1562-1621)

NOSKE, Frits. "Luitcomposites van Jan Pieterszoon Sweelinck,"   **651**
OvKNTV XII (1957):46-48.

TANDLER, Franz

KOCZIRZ, Adolf. "Die Gitarrist Franz Tandler," *Die Gitarre*   **652**
X (1929):5ff.

TARDITI, Paolo (fl. 1610)

MISCHIATI, Oscar. "Tarditi, Paolo," *MGG* 13:126-27.   **653**

TAYLOR, Robert. *See:* **1021.**

TEDESCO, Giovanni. *See:* **358.**

TEGHI, Pierre de [Pietro] (fl. 1550's)

PETROBELLI, Pierluigi, "Teghi, Pierre de," *MGG* 13:174-75.   **654**

TERZI, Giovanni Antonio (fl. 1588)

DARDO, Gianluigi. "Terzi, Giovanni Antonio," *MGG*   **655**
13:255-56.

TESSIER, Charles (fl. 1600's). *See also:* **116.**

LESURE, François. "Tessier, Charles," *MGG* 13:264-65.   **656**

UNGERER, Gustav. "The French Lutenist Charles Tessier and   **657**
the Essex Circle," *Renaissance Quarterly* [=*News*] XXVII/2
(1975):190-203.

TESSIER, Valère (fl. 1600's). *See:* 656.

THURNER, Jacob. *See:* 170.

THYSIUS, Johann (ca. 1578-1653). *See also:* 549.

658   EITNER, Robert. "Das Liederbuch von Thysius," *MfM* XVIII (1886):39-43.

659   LAND, J. P. N. "Het Luitboek van Thysius . . . .," *TVNMg* I (1884): 129-95, 205-64; II (1885):1-56, 109-74, 177-94, 278-350; III (1888):1-57. [Also as *Het Luitboek van Thysius* beschreven en toegelicht door Dr. J. P. N. Land. Repertoire d'un Luthiste hollandois vers les premieres annees du XVIIe siècle. Amsterdam: F. Muller et Cie, 1889. 409p.]

660   RADKE, Hans. "Thysius, Johann," *MGG* 13:382-83.

TOESCHI (Family) (fl. seventeenth and eighteenth century)

661   MÜNSTER, Robert. "Toeschi," *MGG* 13:452-58.

662   ———. "Mannheimer Musiker," *Musica* XV (1961):113-17.

TORRE, Pietro Paolo (fl. 1600's)

663   MARTINOTTI, Sergio. "Torre, Pietro Paolo," *MGG* 13:567.

TROMBONCINO, Bartolomeo (ca. 1470-after 1535)

664   RUBSAMMEN, Walter. "Tromboncino, Bartolomeo," *MGG* 13:723-28.

665   WOLF, Johannes. "Ein alter Lautendruck," *ZIMG* I (1899):29ff.

TURPYN, Francis

666   OBOUSSIER, Phillip. "Turpyn's Book of Lute Songs," *M&L* 34 (1953):145-49.

D'URFEY, Thomas (1653-1723)

667   PERCEVAL, Allen. "D'Urfey, Thomas," *MGG* 3:999-1000.

URSILLO, Fabio (d. 1759)

DEGRADA, Francesco. "Ursillo, Fabio," *MGG* 13:1178-79.   **668**

VALDERRÁBANO, Enrique de (fl. 1550's). *See also:* **1251, 1516, 1730:**
pp. 12-13, 43, 56-57; 1733, 1734.

WARD, John. "Valderrábano, Enrique de," *MGG* 13:1215.   **669**

VALERIUS, Adrianus (d. 1625). *See also:* **506.**

Unsigned (probably Robert Eitner). "Valerius," *MfM* IV   **670**
(1872): 29-30.

ENSCHEDE, J. W. "De Wilhelmus melodie in der Gedenck-   **671**
Clanck van Valerius," *TVNMg* V (1897): 100ff.

KOSSMANN, F. "Die Melodie des 'Wilhelmus von Nassouwe'   **672**
in den Lautenbearbeitung des XVII. Jahrhunderts," *AfMw*
V (1923): 327-31.

RADKE, Hans. "Valerius, Adrianus," *MGG* 13:1236-37.   **673**

SWAEN, A. E. H. "De Engelsche stemmen in Valerius' Gedenck-   **674**
Clanck," *Neophilologus* (Groningen) 30 (1946): 77ff.

VALLET, Nicolas (d. 1626)

BUETENS, Stanley. "Nicolas Vallet's Lute Quartets," *JLSA*   **675**
II (1969): 28-36.

FALK, Marguerite. "De Amsterdamse luitspeler Nicolas Vallet,"   **676**
Mens en Melodie 14 (1959): 140-43.

———. "Die Lautenbücher des Nicolas Vallet," *Schweitzer*   **677**
Musikzeitung 98 (1958): 148-52.

RADKE, Hans. "Vallet, Nicolas," *MGG* 13:1243-44.   **678**

SCHEULEER, D. F. "Het luit boeck van N. Vallet," *TVNMg*   **679**
V (1897): 13-39.

———. "Twee Bijdragen tot de Geschiedenis van N. Vallet,"   **680**
TVNMg VI (1900): 176ff.

VALVASENSI, Lazaro (fl. 1626)

681   SARTORI, Claudio. "Valvasensi, Lazaro," *MGG* 13:1248.

VAN DEN HOVE, Joachim (1575-after 1612)

682   BOETTICHER, Wolfgang. "Hove, Joachim van den," *MGG* 6:789-90.

683   EITNER, Robert. "Joachim van den Hove's Lautenbuch von 1601," *MfM* IX (1877): 59-60.

VAUDRY DE SAIZNEY, Jean Etienne (fl. 1699)

684   VERCHALY, André. "Vaudry de Saizney, Jean Etienne," *MGG* 13:1332.

VECCHI, Orazio (1551-1605)

685   MISCHIATI, Oscar. "Vecchi, Orazio," *MGG* 13:1346-54.

VENTURA, Angelo Benedetto (1781-1856)

686   BONNER, Stephen. *Angelo Benedetto Ventura, Teacher, Inventor and Composer: A Study in English Regency Music.* Bois de Boulogne: Harlow, 1971. 88p.

VERDIER, Pierre (d. 1697)

687   COTE, Roger. "Verdier, Pierre," *MGG* 13:1463-64.

VEROVIO, Simone (d. ca. 1600)

688   SARTORI, Claudio. "Verovio, Claudio," *MGG* 13:1513-14.

VIGNON, Jerome (fl. 1630); Nicolas-François (fl. 1653). See also: 1191.

689   RADKE, Hans. "Vignon," *MGG* 13:1620.

VINCENT, ——? (fl. 1640)

690   VERCHALY, André. "Vincent," *MGG* 13:1653-54.

VIRDUNG, Sebastian (fl. 1510)

FOX, Charles W. "A Pleasant and Very Useful Book (1529)," 691
abstracted in *BAMS* 2 (1937): 22-24. [Translation of Virdung,
Musica getutscht . . . .]

VISÉE, Robert de (1660-1721)

CHILESOTTI, Oscar. "Notes sur le guitariste Robert de Visée," 692
SIMG IX (1907-1908): 62-74.

LESURE, François. "Visée, Mr. de," *MGG* 13:1831-33. 693

VITALI, Filippo (d. 1650)

PRUETT, James W. "Vitali, Filippo," *MGG* 13:1834-36. 694

VIVALDI, Antonio (1680-1743)

EKKER, Rudolf. "Vivaldi, Antonio," *MGG* 13:1849-71. 695

VOSTERMAN, G.

NIJHOFF, W. "En merkwaardig muziekboek te Antwerpen nij 696
Vosterman uitgegeven, 1529," *Het Boek* XXII (1934): 267ff.

WAISSEL, Matthäus (1540-1602)

KLIMA, Josef and Hans RADKE. "Waissel, Matthäus," *MGG* 697
14:138-40.

WEBB, William (d. between 1653-1661). *See also:* 1151.

FLINDELL, Fred. "Webb, William," *MGG* 14:275. 698

FULLER, David. "The Jonsonian Masque and Its Music," 699
M&L 54 (1973): 440-53.

WECKER, Hans Jacob (1528-1586)

RADKE, Hans. "Wecker, Hans Jacob," *MGG* 14:351-52. 700

WEICHENBERGER, Johann Georg (1677-1740)

KLIMA, Josef and Hans RADKE. "Weichenberger, Johann 701
Georg," *MGG* 14:367-68.

WEICHMANN, Johann (1620-1652)

702   BARON, John H. "Weichmann, Johann," *MGG* 14:369-70.

703   KOCZIRZ, Adolf. "Verschollene neudeutsche Lautenisten (Weichmann, Pasch, de Bronikowsky, Raschke)," *AfMw* III (1921):270ff.

WEISS, Johann Sigismund (1690-1748)

704   KLIMA, Josef and Hans RADKE. "Weiss, Johann Sigismund," *MGG* 14:439-40.

WEISS, Sylvius Leopold (1686-1750). *See also:* 2, 12, 111, 1475.

705   KLIMA, Josef and Hans RADKE. "Weiss, Sylvius Leopold," *MGG* 14:437-39.

706   MASON, Wilton E. *The Lute Music of Sylvius Leopold Weiss.* Unpublished Ph.D. diss., University of North Carolina, Chapel Hill, 1949. 124 + 280p.

707   McCONNELL, D. E. "Sylvius Leopold Weiss," *Guitar News* 94 (1967):36-37.

708   NEEMANN, Hans. "Die Lauten-Familie Weiss," *AfMw* IV (1939):157-89.

709   ————. "Wirken und Schaffen des Meisterlautenisten Sylvius Leopold Weiss und seiner Vervandten [mit Beschriebung und Verzeichnis sämtlicher lautenkompositioner der Familie Weiss]," *AfMf* IV (1939).

710   ————. "Zur Bibliographie der Lauten Komponist S. L. Weiss," *Musik im Haus* VII (1928):75ff.

711   PRUSIK, K. *Die Kompositionen des Lautenisten Sylvius Leopold Weiss.* Unpublished Ph.D. diss., Wien, 1924.

712   SCHULZE, Hans-Joachim. "Ein unbekannter Brief von Sylvius Leopold Weiss," *Mf* XX (1968):203-204.

713   SMITH, Douglas Alton. *The Late Sonatas of Sylvius Leopold Weiss.* VIII, 270p. Unpublished Ph.D. diss., Stanford University, 1977.

714   VOLKMANN, H. "Sylvius Leopold Weiss, der letzte Grosse Lautenist," *Die Musik* VI (1906-1907):273ff.

Composers / Performers—Individual Biography

WELD, Dorothy (fl. 1600)

SPENCER, Robert. "The Weld Lute-Book," *LSJ* I (1959):48-57.　　715

WERT, Giaches de (1535-1596)

MacCLINTOCK, Carol. "Two Lute Intabulations of Wert's　　716
'Cara La Vita'," *Festschrift APEL*, pp. 93-99.

WHITE, Robert (1530-1574)

SPECTOR, Irwin. "The Music of Robert White," *Consort* 23　　717
(1966):100-108.

―――. *The Instrumental Music of Robert White*. Madison:　　718
A-R Editions, Inc., 1972. 110p.

―――. *Robert White, Composer Between Two Eras*.　　719
Unpublished Ph.D. diss., Yale University, 1952.

WHITNEY, Geoffrey

BRETT, Philip. "Musicae Modernae Laus: Geoffrey Whitney's　　720
Tribute to the Lute and Its Players," *LSJ* VII (1965):40.

WILLAERT, Adrian (1485-1562)

ORTNER, Oswald. *Adrian Willaert's Lautenbearbeitungen von*　　721
Madrigalen des Philippo Verdelot. Unpublished Ph.D. diss.,
Wien, 1939.

VERSTENBERG, Walter. "Willaert, Adrian," *MGG* 14:662-76.　　722

WILSON, John (1595-1674). *See also:* **439, 1410, 1412.**

CRUM, M. A. "A Manuscript of John Wilson's Songs," *The*　　723
Library X 5th ser. (1955):55-57.

CUTTS, John P. "John Wilson and Lovelace's 'The Rose'," *Notes*　　724
and Queries 198 (1953):153ff.

―――. "Seventeenth-Century Lyrics," *MD* X (1956):141-209.　　725

DUCKLES, Vincent. "Wilson, John," *MGG* 14:701-704.　　726

―――. "The 'Curious' Art of John Wilson (1595-1674): An　　727
Introduction to His Songs and Lute Music," *JAMS* (1954):93-112.

Construction

728   HENDERSON, Hubert P. *The Vocal Music of John Wilson.*
Unpublished Ph.D. diss., University of North Carolina, Chapel
Hill, 1962. 388p. UM 63-03495.

729   RIMBAULT, E. F. *Who was Jack Wilson?* London: J. R. Smith,
1846. 16p.

730   STEVENS, Denis. "Seventeenth-Century Italian Instrumental Music
in the Bodleian Library," *AMl* XXVI (1954): 67-74.

WYATT, Thomas. *See also:* **1169.**

731   GOMBOSI, Otto and M. BUKOFZER. "Blame Not My Lute,"
Renaissance News VIII (1955): 12-14.

732   LONG, John M. "Blame Not Wyatt's Lute," *Renaissance News*
VII (1954): 127-30.

733   MUMFORD, I. L. "Musical Settings of the Poems of Sir Thomas
Wyatt," *M&L* 37 (1956): 315-22.

WOLTZ, Johann (d. 1618)

734   HUG, Manfred. "Woltz, Johann," *MGG* 14:840-41.

WYSSENBACH, Rudolf (1527-before 1572)

735   RADKE, Hans. "Wyssenbach, Rudolf," *MGG* 14:920-22.

ZECHNER, Georg (d. 1713)

736   RIEDEL, Friedrich. "Zechner, Georg," *MGG* 14:1037-39.

CONSTRUCTION

737 ABBOTT, Djilda and E. SEGERMAN. "On Lute Bridges and Frets,"
EM 3/3 (1975): 295.

738 ————. "On the Sound of Early 16th-Century Lutes," *EM* 3/4
(1975): 417.

739 ————. "Strings in the 16th and 17th Centuries," *GSJ* XXVII
(1974): 48-73.

Construction

ARNAUT, Henri. *Instruments de musique du XVIe siècle. Les traités d'Henri Arnaut de Zwolle et de divers anonymes.* Edités et commentés par G. le Cerf. Paris: Editions A. Picard, 1932. 58p.   **740**

————. Latin Tract with diagram of the Lute from ca. 1450. Facs. with French transl. in *Instruments de Musique de XVe siècle.* Paris: Picard, 1952.   **741**

BACHORIK, Joan. *Lute Making.* New York: Privately Printed, 1974. 58p.   **742**

BALDINI, Ugo. *Note di Tecnologia construttiva su la chitarra.* Modena and Milan, 2nd ed., 1957.   **743**

BOIVIE, H. "Några Svenska Lut- och Fiolmakare unter 1700-Talet," *Fataburen*, 1921, pp. 51-73.   **744**

BORSO, Pietro. *La liuteria e la scuola del violina in Toscana.* Pisa: Tipografia editrice Pacini, 1930. 76p.   **745**

BUETENS, Stanley. "On Fretting a Lute," *JLSA* III (1970): 53-63.   **746**

BURNE, R. E. *Lute Construction* [title indefinite]. E. P. Dutton, forthcoming.   **747**

COOPER, Robert S. *Lute Construction with a Short History of the Lute by Suzanne Bloch.* Savannah, Georgia: Carriage House, 1963.   **748**

DOMBOIS, Eugen M. "Correct and Easy Fret Placement," *JLSA* VI (1973): 30-32.   **749**

EDWARDS, David. "A Geometrical Construction for a Lute Profile," *LSJ* XV (1973): 48-49.   **750**

GILL, Donald. "James Talbot's Manuscript," *GSJ* XV (1962): 60-69.   **751**

HARWOOD, Ian. "Correspondence," [on Kottick article *GSJ* (1973): 72-83] *GSJ* XXVII (1974): 158-60.   **752**

————. "A Fifteenth-Century Lute Design," *LSJ* II (1960): 3-8.   **753**

Construction

754   HELLWIG, Friedman. "An Example of Lute Restoration," *GSJ* XXIII (1970): 64-68.

755   ———. "Lute Construction in the Renaissance and the Baroque," *GSJ* XXVII (1974): 21-30.

756   ———. "Lute-Making in the Late 15th and 16th Centuries," *LSJ* XIV (1974): 24-38.

757   ———. "On the Construction of the Lute Belly," *GSJ* XXI (1968): 129-45.

758   JAHNEL, F. *Die Gitarre und ihr Bau. Technologie von Gitarre, Laute, Mandoline, Sister, Tanbur und Saite.* Frankfurt, 1963. 256p.

759   KOTTICK, Edward L. "Building a 15th-Century Lute," *GSJ* XXVI (1973): 72-83.

760   ———. "Communication," [reply to R. Lundberg, re: no. 783]. *JLSA* VIII (1975): 103.

761   LAYER, Adolf. "Die Anfänge der Lautenbaukunst in Schwaben," *Mf* 9 (1956): 190-93.

762   LESURE, François. "La facture instrumentale à Paris au Seizième siècle," *GSJ* VII (1954): 11-52; X (1957): 87-88.

763   LUNDBERG, Robert. "Sixteenth- and Seventeenth-Century Lute-Making," *JSLA* VII (1974): 31-50.

764   LÜTGENDORFF, W. L. *Die Geigen und Lautenmacher vom Mittlealter bis zur Gegenwart, nach dem besten Quellen bearbeitet . . . .* Frankfurt am Main: Frankfurter Verlags-Anstalt, 1922. Reprinted New York: Broude Bros., 1967.

765   MÖLLER, Richard. *Laute, Viola da Gamba, Viola da Braccio.* Beihefte zum Monatsschrift, *Die Laute.* Wolfenbüttel: Georg Kallmeyer Verlag, 1918. 31p.

766   POULTON, Diana. "Lute Stringing in the Light of Surviving Tablatures," *LSJ* VI (1964): 14ff.

PRYNNE, Michael. "James Talbot's Manuscript. IV Plucked Strings-   **767**
    The Lute Family," *GSJ* XIV (1961): 52-68.

————. "Lute Bellies and Barring," *LSJ* VI (1964): 7-12.   **768**

————. "Some Remarks on the Lute Forgeries," *LSJ* (1961): 17-21.   **769**

————. "Some Remarks on Old Lutes," *LSJ* I (1959): 23-30.   **770**

————. "An Unrecorded Lute by Hans Frei," *GSJ* II (1949): 47-51.   **771**

ROTTMAN, Kurt. "Historical Lute Bellies from the Standpoint of   **772**
    Modern Statics and Acoustics," *GSJ* XXVI (1973): 25-28.

SALAS VIU, Vincente. "Viejos y nuevos laudes," *Revista Musical*   **773**
    Chilena (1945) , pp. 22-25.

SOMOGYI, Erwin. "Lute Construction," *Guitar Player* 10 (1976):   **774**
    12, 44, 46, 48, 50.

SCHUSTER, F. "Zur Geschichte des Gitarrenbaus in Deutschland,"   **775**
    Die Gitarre X/11-12 (1929).

WECKERLIN, J. B. "Discourse non plus melancoliques que divers,   **776**
    de choses memement qui appartiennent à Notre France," in
    Nouveau Musicana. Garnier Freres, 1887, pp. 103-20. [Quotes
    an anon. treatise on fretting (1556)] . *See:* 974:15 fn. 28.

WILLIAM G. "Lute Construction and Playing," *EM* 3/2 (1975): 177,   **777**
    179. [Reply by I. Harwood *EM* (1975), pp. 179-80, 183, 185.]

EDITIONS

ALBERT DE RIPPE. *Oeuvres d'Albert de Rippe.* I: Fantaisies.   **778**
    II: Motets, Chansons. Edited by J-M Vaccaro. Paris: CNRS,
    1972, 1974.

ALLISON, Richard. *The Psalmes of David in Meter . . . .* London,   **779**
    1599. Facsimile edition. Menston: Scolar Press, Ltd., 1968.

Editions

780 ATTAIGNANT, Pierre. *Preludes, Chansons and Dances for Lute (1529-1530)*. Edited by D. Heartz. Neuilly-Sur-Seine: Société de Musique D'Autrefois, 1964.

781 ATTEY, John. *The First Booke of Ayres*, London, 1622. Edited by D. Greer. Facsimile edition. Menston: Scolar Press, Ltd., 1967.

782 BACH, J. S. *Drei Lautenkompositionen in zeitgenossischen tabulatur.* Edited by Hans J. Schultze. Leipzig: Zentral Antiquariat der DDR, 1975.

783 ————. [J.] *Sebastian Bach's Kompositionen für die Laute.* Edited by Wilhelm Tappert. Berlin, 1901. 6p. [Originally appeared in *Redenden Kunst* VI.] *See also:* **78.**

784 BAILLEUX, Antoine. *Methode de guitarre par musique et tablature.* Geneva: Minkoff, 1971. [Includes Lemoine, A. M. *Nouvelle Methode . . .* , 1790].

785 BALLARD, Robert. *Première Livre, 1611.* Edited by A. Souris and S. Spycket. Introduction by M. Rollin. Paris: CNRS, 1963.

786 ————. *Deuxième Livre, 1614 et Pièces Diverses.* Edited by A. Souris and S. Spycket. Paris: CNRS, 1964.

BARBETTA, G. C. *See:* **108.**

787 BARLEY, William. *New Booke of Tabliture, 1596.* [= *Lute Music of Shakespear's Time.*] Edited and transcribed by Wilburn Newcomb. University Park, Pennsylvania: Pennsylvania State University Press, 1966.

788 BARON, Ernst G. *Fantasia for Lute.* Edited by A. Quadt. London: Boosey and Hawkes, n.d.

789 BARTLETT, John. *A Booke of Ayres*, London, 1606. Edited by D. Greer. Facsimile edition. Menston: Scolar Press, Ltd., 1967.

790 BESARD, Jean-Baptiste. *Jean Baptiste Besardus: Instructionen für Laute 1610 und 1617.* Mit einem Nachwort Versehen von Peter Päffgen. Neuss/Rhein: GbR Junghänel, Päffgen, Schäffer, 1974. 51p.

————. *Thesaurus Harmonicus* (*1603*). Facsimile edition. Geneva: **791**
Minkoff, 1975.

————. *Oeuvres pour luth seul.* Edited by A. Souris. Paris: CNRS,   **792**
1969. XLII + 165p.

BATCHELAR, Daniel *Daniel Batchelar, Selected Works.* Edited by   **793**
Martin Long. London: Oxford University Press, 1972.

BITTNER, Jacques. *Pièces de Luth* (*1682*). Instituto Pro Arte   **794**
Testudenis. Neuss-Rhein: GbR Junghänel, Päffgen, Schäffer,
1974.

BOARD, Margaret. *The Board Lute Book.* Facsimile edition. Leeds: **795**
Boethius Press, 1975.

BOSSINENSIS, Franciscus. *See:* **134.**

BOTTEGARI, Ercole. *See:* **134.**

BURWELL, Mary. *Burwell Lute Tutor.* Facsimile edition with   **796**
introduction by R. Spencer. Leeds: Boethius Press, 1974.

CAMPION, Thomas. *The Description of a Masque in Honor of Lord*   **797**
Hayes, 1607. Facsimile edition. Menston: Scolar Press, Ltd.

————. *The Description of a Maske Presented at the Marriage of the*   **798**
Earle of Somerset, 1614. Facsimile edition. Menston: Scolar
Press, Ltd., 1973.

————. *The Third and Fourth Booke of Ayres*, 1618. Facsimile   **799**
edition. Menston: Scolar Press, Ltd., 1970.

————. *Two Books of Ayres*, 1613. Facsimile edition. Menston: **800**
Scolar Press, Ltd., 1973.

————. *The Songs from Rosseter's Book of Airs* (*1601*). ELS,   **801**
ser. I, vol. 14 (1922) vol. 13 (1922); rev. ed. T. Dart (1965).
London: Stainer and Bell.

CAPIROLA, Vincenzo. *Compositione de Meser Vincenzo Capirola*   **802**
(*1571*). Edited by O. Gombosi. Neuilly-sur-Seine: Société de
Musique D'Autrefois, 1955. 185p.

Editions

803 CARARA, Michel. *Michel Carara's Intabolatura di Liuto, 1585.* Florence: Biblioteca degli Historiae Musicae Cultures, 1957. 4p.

804 CATO, Diomedes. *Diomedes Cato. Preludia, fantazje, tance i madrygaly.* Vol. I. Edited by Piotr Poźniak. Warszawa: Polskie Wydawnictwo Muzyczne, 1970. [Introduction in Polish and English.]

805 ———. *Diomedes Cato. Preludia, fantazje, tance i madrygaly.* Vol. 2. Warszawa: Polskie Wydawnictwo Muzyczne, 1973.

806 CAVENDISH, Michael. *14 Ayres in Tableturie to the Lute,* London 1598. Facsimile edition. Menston: Scolar Press, Ltd., 1971.

807 CERTON, Pierre. *Guillaume Morlaye: Psaumes de Pierre Certon réduits pour chant et luth.* Introduction by François Lesure, transcription by R. de Morcourt. Paris: CNRS, 1957. 76p.

808 CHANCY, François. *Oeuvres de Chancy, Bouvier, Belleville, Dubuisson, Chevalier.* Paris: CNRS, 1967.

809 COPERARIO, Giovanni. *Funeral Tears (1606) Songs of Mourning (1613) The Masque of Squires (1614).* ELS, vol. 17, ser. 1. Edited by G. Hendrie and T. Dart. London: Stainer and Bell, n.d.

810 ———. *Funeral Teares, for the Death of Right Honorable, the Earle of Devonshire . . . ,* London 1606. Facsimile edition. Menston: Scolar Press, Ltd., 1970.

811 ———. *Songs of Mourning . . . ,* London, 1613. Facsimile edition Menston: Scolar Press, Ltd., 1970.

812 CORBETTA, Francesco. *La Guitarre Royalle (1671).* Facsimile edition. Geneva: Minkoff, 1975.

813 CORKINE, William. *Ayres to Sing and Play to the Lute . . . ,* London, 1610. Facsimile edition. Menston: Scolar Press, Ltd., 1970.

814 ———. *The Second Booke of Ayres . . . ,* London, 1612. Facsimile edition. Menston: Scolar Press, Ltd., 1970.

DALZA, Joan Ambrosio. *See:* **192.**

DANYEL, John. *Songs for the Lute, Viol and Voice*, London 1606. Edited **815**
by D. Greer. Facsimile edition. Menston: Scolar Press, Ltd., 1970.

DOWLAND, John. *The Collected Lute Music of John Dowland.* **816**
Transcribed and edited by Diana Poulton and Basil Lam.
London: Faber Music, 1974. XVI + 317p.

———. *The First Booke of Songes or Ayres*, London 1597. Facsimile **817**
edition. Menston: Scolar Press, Ltd., 1968.

———. *The First Book of Ayres* (*1597, 1600, 1603, 1606, 1613*). **818**
Edited by E. Fellowes. ELS, ser. 1 (1920), rev. 1965, T. Dart.
London: Stainer and Bell.

———. *The Second Booke of Songes or Ayres*, London 1600. Edited by **819**
D. Poulton. Facsimile edition. Menston: Scolar Press, Ltd., 1970.

———. *The Second Booke of Songs* (*1600*). Edited by E. Fellowes. **820**
(1922) rev. T. Dart (1968). London: Stainer and Bell.

———. *The Third and Last Booke of Songs or Ayres*, London 1603. **821**
Facsimile edition. Menston: Scolar Press, Ltd.

———. *The Third Book of Airs* (*1603*). ELS, vols. 10-11. Edited **822**
by E. Fellowes (1923), rev. ed. T. Dart and D. Scott (1969).
London: Stainer and Bell.

———. *A Pilgrimes Solace . . .* , London, 1612. Facsimile edition. **823**
Menston: Scolar Press, Ltd., 1970.

———. *A Pilgrims Solace* (*Fourth Book of Airs 1612*). ELS, vol. **824**
12 rev. ed. T. Dart. London: Stainer and Bell, n.d.

DOWLAND, Robert. *A Musicall Banquet . . .* , London, 1610. **825**
Facsimile edition. Menston: Scolar Press, Ltd., 1969. 23p.

———. *Varietie of Lute-Lessons.* A lithographic facsimile of the **826**
original edition of 1610, with an introduction by E. Hunt.
London: Schott, 1957.

DUFAUT. *Oeuvres de Defaut.* Introduction by Monique Rollin. **827**
Paris: CNRS, 1965.

828 *Elizabethan Popular Music.* General editor, D. Lumsden. London: Oxford University Press.

829 FERRABOSCO, Alphonso. *Ayres and Songs,* London 1609. Edited by D. Greer. Facsimile edition. Menston: Scolar Press, Ltd., 1970.

830 FORDE, Thomas. *Airs to the Lute,* from *Musicke of Sundrie Kindes* (*1607*), ELS vol. 3. Edited by E. Fellowes (1921), rev. ed. by T. Dart (1966). London: Stainer and Bell.

831 ————. *Musicke of Sundrie Kindes,* London 1607. Edited by D. Greer. Facsimile edition. Menston: Scolar Press, Ltd., 1971.

832 FRANCESCO DA MILAN. *Francesco da Milano: Opere complete per liuto.* Transcribed and edited by Ruggero Chiesa. Milano: Suvini-Zerboni, 1971. 2 vols.

833 ————. *The Lute Music of Francesco Canova da Milano* (*1497-1543*). Edited by Arthur J. Ness. Cambridge, Massachusetts: Harvard University Press, 1970. 473p.

834 GALILEI, Vincenzo. *Two Lute duets from Il Fronimo.* Edited with tablature facsimile by J. Iodone. New York: Associated Music Publishers. n.d.

GALLOT, Jacques. *See:* 327.

835 GAULTIER, Denis. *Pièces de Luth . . . sur trois différents modes nouveau,* (*1670*). Includes *Livre de tablature des pièces de luth sur plusieurs différents modes . . .* (*1680*). Facsimile edition. Geneva: Minkoff, 1975.

836 ————. *La Rhetorique des Dieux, et autre pièces de luth de Denis Gaultier.* Facsimile edition with introduction by André Tessier. Paris: Société française de musicologie, 1932. 53 + 145p.

837 GAULTIER, Ennemond. *Oeuvres du vieux Gaultier.* Introduction and study by Monique Rollin. Paris: CNRS, 1966.

838 GERLE, Hans. *Musica teutsch auf die Instrument ser grossen und kleinen Geygen, auch Lautten . . . .* Facsimile reprint of 1532 edition. New York: Broude Bros., 1967.

GREAVES, Thomas. *Songes of Sundrie Kindes* . . . , London 1604. Edited   **839**
by D. Greer. Facsimile edition. Menston: Scolar Press, Ltd., 1971.

GUERAU, Francisco. *A Transcription of Poema Harmonico by*   **840**
Francisco Guerau for Baroque Guitar. Transcription by Janis
Stevenson. Unpublished Master's thesis, San Jose State University,
1974. 282p.

HANDFORD, George. *Ayres to be Sunge to the Lute*, London 1609. Edited   **841**
by D. Greer. Facsimile edition. Menston: Scolar Press, Ltd., 1970.

HAYDN, Joseph. *Cassation in C Major for Lute, Violin and 'Cello.*   **842**
Edited by Hans Neemann. Berlin: Verlag Christian Vieweg. n.d..

HOLBORNE, Anthony. *The Complete Works of Anthony Holborne.*   **843**
Vol. 1—Music for Lute and Bandora. Edited by Masakata
Kanazawa. Cambridge, Massachusetts: Harvard University Press,
1967.

————. *The Complete Works of Anthony Holborne.* Vol. 2—Music   **844**
for Cittern. Edited by Masakata Kanazawa. Cambridge,
Massachusetts: Harvard University Press, 1973. 179p.

HUME, Tobias. *Captain Hume's Poeticall Musicke*, London 1607. Edited   **845**
by F. Traficante. Facsimile edition. Menston: Scolar Press, Ltd., 1969.

————. *The First Parts of Ayres*, London 1605. Facsimile edition.   **846**
Menston: Scolar Press, Ltd., 1970-.

JOBIN, Bernard. *See:* **398**.

JOHNSON, Robert. *Complete Works for Solo Lute.* Edited by A.   **847**
Sundermann. London: Oxford University Press, 1972. 51p.

JONES, Robert. *The First Booke of Songs and Ayres*, London 1600. Edited   **848**
by D. Greer. Facsimile edition. Menston: Scolar Press, Ltd., 1970.

————. *The Second Book of Songs and Ayres*, London 1601. Edited by   **849**
D. Greer. Facsimile edition. Menston: Scolar Press, Ltd., 1971.

————. *The Muses Gardin, or The Fifth Booke of Ayres*, London 1610.   **850**
Edited by D. Greer. Facsimile edition. Menston: Scolar Press,
Ltd., 1970.

851 ————. *Ultimum Vale, or The Third Booke of Ayres*, London 1605. Edited by D. Greer. Facsimile edition. Menston: Scolar Press, Ltd., 1971.

852 KOCZIRZ, Adolf, ed. *Österreichische Lautenmusik im XVI Jahrhundert ...zwischen 1650 und 1720.* DTÖ vol. 37.

853 LAUFFENSTEINER, Wolff Jacob. *Zwei Praludien und fünf Partien für Laute.* Edited by Hans Radke. Musik Alter Meister series, heft 30. Graz: Akademische Druck- und Verlagsanstalt, 1973. XIII + 36p.

854 LEIGHTON, William. *The Tear of Lamentations of a Sorrowful Soul (1614), by William Leighton.* Unpublished Ph.D. diss., St Andrews (England), 1967.

855 LeROY, Adrian. *Première livre de tablature de luth (1551).* Edited and transcribed by A. Souris and R. de Morcourt. Introduction by M. Rollin. Paris: CNRS, 1961.

856 MACE, Thomas. *Musick's Monument*, 1676. Facsimile edition. Vol. 1 (and vol. 2= commentary and transcription). Paris: CNRS, 1966. 272p.

857 MASON, George. *The Ayres That Were Sung and Played at Brougham Castle (1618).* Facsimile edition. Edited by D. Greer. Menston: Scholar Press, Ltd., 1970.

858 MAYNARD, John. *The Twelve Wonders of the World (1611-1612).* Facsimile edition. Edited by Ian Harwood. Menston: Scolar Press, Ltd., 1970.

859 MESANGEAU, René. *Oeuvres de René Mesangeau.* Edited and transcribed by A. Souris with an introduction by M. Rollin. Paris: CNRS, 1971. 36 + 58p.

860 MILAN, Luys. *Libro de Musica de Vihuela de Mano (1536).* Facsimile edition. Geneva: Minkoff, 1975.

861 ————. *Luis Milan, Musikalische Werk.* Edited by Leo Schrade. Publicationen älterer Musik, vol. 2. Leipzig, 1927. Reprinted Hildesheim: G. Olms, 1967.

MORLAYE, Guillaume. *See:* **807.**

MORLEY, Thomas. *The First Booke of Airs*, London 1600. Facsimile 862
edition. Edited by D. Greer. Menston: Scolar Press, Ltd., 1970.

————. *The First Book of Airs*, London 1600. Edited by E. Fellowes 863
(1932) rev. ed. by T. Dart (1965). ELS vol. 16. London: Stainer
and Bell.

————. *The First Book of Consort-Lessons* for Treble- and Bass-Viols, 864
Flute, Lute, Cittern and Pandora by Thomas Morley. Edited with
an introduction by Sydney Beck, New York: New York Public
Library, 1959.

MORPHY, Don Guillermo, ed. *Die spanischen Lautenmeister des* 865
XVI Jahrhunderts. Leipzig: Breitkopf und Härtel, 1902. 2 vols.
Translated into French by Malherbe and reprinted by Broude
Bros., 1967.

MURCIA, Santiago. *See:* 522.

MYNSHALL. *The Mynshall Lute Book.* Facsimile edition. Leeds: 866
Boethius Press, 1974.

NARVÁEZ, Luys de. *Twelve Selections from Delphin de Musica* 867
(*1538*). Edited and transcribed by S. Buetens. Redondo Beach:
Instrumenta Antiqua Publications, 1975.

————. *Vihuelistas Españoles del Siglo XVI. Narváez, El Delphin* 868
de Musica, 1538. Edited by E. Martinez-Torner. Madrid: Union
Musical Española, 1965.

NEWSIDLER, Hans. *Hans Newsidler: Ein Newgeordent Künstlich* 869
Lautenbuch, 1536. Institutio Pro Arte Testudenis. Neuss/Rhein:
GbR Junghänel-Pättgen-Schäffer, 1974. 173p.

PERRINE, ——. *Livre de musique pour le lut, contenant une methode* 870
nouvelle et facile pour apprendre a toucher le lut sur les notes de
la musique, (*1679*). Facsimile reprint. Geneva: Minkoff, 1973.
58p.

PILKINGTON, Francis. *The First Booke of Ayres*, London 1605. Edited 871
by D. Greer. Facsimile edition. Menston: Scolar Press, Ltd., 1969.

Editions

872 ————. *First Book of Songs or Airs* (*1605*). Edited by E. Fellowes, ELS vol. 7 (1922), vol. 15 (1925). Rev, ed. T. Dart. London: Stainer and Bell, 1970.

873 REUSNER, Esaias. *Esaias Reusner and Sylvius Leopold Weiss*. Das Erbe Deutsche Musik, vol. 12. Frankfurt an Main: Henry Litolff Verlag.

874 ROBINSON, Thomas. *The Schoole of Musicke, 1603.* Edited and transcribed by D. Lumsden. Paris: CNRS, 1972.

875 ROSSEITER, Philip. *A Book of Ayres*, London 1601. Edited by D. Greer. Facsimile edition. Menston: Scolar Press, Ltd., 1970.

876 ————. *Songs from Rosseter's Book of Airs* (*1601*). ELS vols. 8-9. Edited by E. Fellowes (1922) rev. ed. T. Dart. London: Stainer and Bell, 1966.

877 SAMPSON (Tollemache) Lute Book. *The Sampson Lute-Book.* Facsimile edition. Leeds: Boethius Press, 1974.

878 SANZ, Gaspar. *Instrucción de Música sobre la guitarra española* (*1697*). Facsimile reprint. Geneva: Minkoff, 1975.

879 ————. *Instrucción de música . . . .* Edited by Luis Garcia-Abrines. Zaragoza: Institution Fernando el Catolica de la Exema, Disputación Provencial (C. S. I. S.), 1952, 1966.

880 ————. *Gaspar Sanz: Instrucción de música sobre la guitarra española* (*1674*). Edited, translated and transcribed by Robert Strizich. London: Schott, forthcoming.

881 SEIDEL, Ferdinand. *12 Minuets for Lute.* Edited with facsimile by A. Quadt. London: Boosey and Hawkes, n.d.

882 SPINACINO, Francesco. Schmidt, Henry L. *The First Printed Lute Books: Francesco Spinacino's Intavolatura de Lauto, Libro primo and Libro secondo* (*Venezia, Petrucci, 1507*). Unpublished Ph.D. diss., University of North Carolina, Chapel Hill, 1969. 2 vols. UM 70-03308.

883 TERZI, Joannis Antoni. *Joannis Antoni Terzi. Opera Intavolatura di Liuto, Libro Primo* (*1593*). Bergamo: Editioni Monumenta Bergomensia, 1969.

THURNER, J. *Das Lautenbüchlein des Jacob Thurner.* Edited by   **884**
Rudolf Flotzinger. Graz: Akademische Druck- und Verlagsanstalt,
1971.

THYSIUS, Johann. *See:* **659**.

TURPIN. *The Turpin Lute-Book.* Introduction by R. Rastall. Leeds: **885**
Boethius Press, 1974.

VALLET, Nicolas. *Les Secrets des Muses. Première Livre, 1615. Second*   **886**
Livre, 1619. Edited and transcribed by A. Souris with introduction
by M. Rollin. Paris: CNRS, 1970. XLII + 260p.

VAUMESNIL, ――. *Oeuvres de Vaumesnil, Edinthon, Perrichon, Raël,*   **887**
Montbuysson, LaGrotte, Saman, LaBarré. Edited and transcribed
by A Souris, M. Rollin and J-M Vaccaro. Paris: CNRS, 1975
60 + 152p.

VERCHALY, André, (ed.) *Airs de Cour pour Voix et Luth, 1603-1643.*   **888**
Paris: Heugel et Cie, 1961.

Weiner Lautenmusik im 18. Jahrhundert. Edited by Karl Schnurl.   **889**
DTÖ vol. 84. Graz: Akademische Druck- und Verlagsanstalt,
1966.

WEISS, Sylvius Leopold. *Intavolatura di Liuto.* Edited by R. Chiesa.   **890**
Milano: Suvini-Zerboni, 1968. 2 vols. *See also:* **706, 873**.

WHITE, Robert. *See:* **718**.

GUITAR

AZPIAZU, J. de. *The Guitar and Guitarists from the Beginning to the*   **891**
Present Day. London, 1960.

B., L. "Musik zur Gitarre oder Laute," *Der Merker* I (1910):345-48.   **892**

BELLOW, Alexander. *The Illustrated History of the Guitar.* New   **893**
York, 1970.

894 BERAU, F. "Zum Stand der Gitarristik in Russland," *ZfdG* IV/10+ (1925).

895 BIERNATH, E. *Die Gitarre seit dem dritten Jahrtausend vor Christus.* Berlin: A. Hoack, 1907.

896 BLANCHARD, Henri. "Les Guitaristes," *Revue et Gazette Musicale de Paris* (1842).

897 BOETTICHER, Wolfgang and H. HICKMAN. "Gitarre," *MGG* 5:174-202.

898 BONE, Philip J. *The Guitar and Mandolin: Biographies of Celebrated Players and Composers.* 2nd. edition. London, 1954. Repr. Schott, 1972.

899 BOWLES, Edmund. "The Guitar in Medieval Literature," *GR* 29 (1966): 3-7.

900 BUEK, Fritz. *Die Gitarre und ihre Meister.* Berlin, 1926.

901 CARFAGNA, Carlo. *Dizionario chitarristico italiano.* Ancona: Bèrben, 1968. 97p.

902 ———. *Profilo storico della chitara.* Ancona: Bèrben, 1966. 106p.

903 CHARNASSÉ, Hélène. "La Guitare," *Connaisance des Arts* (November, 1965).

904 CHASE, Gilbert. "Guitar and Vihuela: A Clarification," *BAMS* VI (1940): 13ff.

905 CHILESOTTI, Oscar. "Intavolature di chitarra, appunti," *Le Chronache Musicali,* I (1900): 17ff.

906 CIURLO, E. Fausto. "Cenni sulle ricerche della chitarra e del liuto," *IFr* I/3 (June, 1973): 16-24.

907 CONTRERAS, N. S. *La Guitarra, sus antecendentes históricos y biografias de ejecutantes célebres.* Buenos Aires, 1927. 135p.

908 DANNER, Peter. L'Adattamento della musica barocca per chitarra all'esecuzione moderna," *IFr* I/7 (April, 1974): 11-20.

————. "Bibliography of Guitar Tablatures 1546-1764," *JLSA*   **909**
V (1972): 40-51.

————. "An Update to the Bibliography of Guitar Tablatures," *JLSA*   **910**
VI (1973): 33-36.

DELL'ARA, Mario. "La chitarra vel 1700," *IFr* (July, 1975): 6-14.   **911**

DIDEROT, Denis and D'Alembert. "Guitarre," *Encyclopédie, ou*   **912**
Dictionairre raisonné des Sciences et des arts et des metiers. 3rd
edition. Geneva, 1779. Vol. 16, p. 835ff.

ELORRIAGA, L. "The Guitar," *GR* 8 (1949): 35-39.   **913**

FEDERHOFER, Hellmut. "Ein Angelica- und Gitarren-tabulatur aus   **914**
der zweiten Hälfte des 17. Jahrhunderts," in *Festschrift WIORA*,
pp. 313-16.

FREEDMAN, R. S. "Evolution of the Guitar," *Music Journal*   **915**
27 (1969): 62-65.

FRYKLUND, O. "Bidrag till gitarristen," *Slöjd och Ton* XIII   **916**
(1931): 73ff.

GEIRINGER, Karl. "Der Instrumentenname 'Quinterne' und die   **917**
Mittelalterlichen Bezeichnungen der Guitarre, Mandola und das
Colascione," *AfMw* VI (1924): 103-10.

GILL, Donald. "The Stringing of the Five-Course Baroque Guitar,"   **918**
EM 3/4 (October, 1975): 370-71.

GIORDANO, M. *Contributo allo studio della chitarra, introduzione*   **919**
e ségiuto a tutti i metodi. Milano, 1936.

————. "La chitarra in Sardegna," *Il Plettro* XXIX (1933-1934): 7ff.   **920**

GLADDING, Bessie A. "Music as a Social Force During the English   **921**
Commonwealth and Restoration (1649-1700)," *MQ* XV
(1929): 506-21.

GODWIN, Jocelyn. "Eccentric Forms of the Guitar," *JLSA* VII   **922**
(1974): 90-102.

923   GOMBOSI, O. "Ad vocem 'cithara, citarista'," *AMl* IX (1937): 55-57.

924   HAMILTON, Mary Neal. *Music in Eighteenth Century Spain.* Urbana: University of Illinois, 1937. pp. 146-56.

925   HEARTZ, Daniel. "Parisian Music Publishing Under Henry II A Propos of Four Recently Discovered Guitar Books," *MQ* XLVI (1960): 448ff.

926   HECK, Thomas F. *The Birth of the Classic Guitar and Its Cultivation in Vienna, Reflected in the Career and Compositions of Mauro Giuliani (d. 1829).* Unpublished Ph.D. diss., Yale University, 1970. UM 71-16246.

927   ————. "The Role of Italy in the Early History of the Classic Guitar: A Sidelight on the House of Ricordi, I," *GR* 34 (1971): 1-6.

928   HEIMER, B. A. "Något om Guitarren," *Slöjd och Ton* VI (1937): 5ff.

929   HENZE, Bruno. *Die Gitarre und ihre Meister des 18. und 19. Jahrhunderts.* Berlin: A Köster, 1920. 48p.

930   HERTZOG, E. "Duet Music for Guitar and a Keyboard Instrument," *Guitar News* no. 102, pp. 28-30.

931   HUBER, Jacques. *Origines et technique de la guitare.* Lausanne, 1968. 210p.

932   HUDSON, Richard A. "The Concept of Mode in Italian Guitar Music During the First Half of the 17th Century," *AMl* XLII/3-4 (1970): 163-83.

933   ————. *The Development of Italian Keyboard Variations on the Passacoglio and Ciaccona from Guitar Music in the Seventeenth Century.* Unpublished Ph.D. diss., University of California, Los Angeles, 1967. UM 68-00219.

934   ————. "The Music in Italian Tablatures for the Five-Course Spanish Guitar," *JLSA* IV (1971): 21-42.

935   HUTTIG, H. E. "The Guitar Maker and His Techniques," *GR* 28 (1965).

936   KASHA, Michael. "A New Look at the History of the Classic Guitar," *GR* 30 (1967): 3-12.

951   LESURE, François. "La Guitare en France au XVIe siècle," *MD* IV
      (1950): 187-95.

952   MARSCHKJEWITCH, W. "Die Siebensaitige Gitarre. Eine Erwiderung,"
      Musik im Haus VI/1 (1926).

953   MUNOZ, R. *Historia de la guitarra.* Buenos Aires, 1930.

954   MURPHY, M. *Guitar Music in Spain and Italy in the 17th Century.* Ph.D.
      diss., London (RHC), forthcoming.

955   NORLIND, Tobias. "Lyra und Kithara in der Antike," *STMf* XVI
      (1934): 76-98.

956   PUJOL, E. "Guitare," in *Encyclopédie de la Musique.* Edited by A.
      Lavignac, 1913-1931, pp. 1997-2035.

957   ———. *La guitarra e su historia.* Buenos Aires, 1932.

958   REMNANT, Mary. "The Gittern in English Medieval Art," *GSJ* 18
      (1965): 104-109.

959   RISCHEL, T. "Zur Geschichte der Gitarre in Dänemark," *Die Gitarre*
      XII/9-10 (1931).

960   SAINZ DE LA MAZA, Regino. *La guitarra y su historia.* Madrid: Ateneo,
      1955.

961   SAMPAYO RIBEIRO, M. de. *As guitarras de Alcácer, e a guitarra
      portugesa.* Lisbon, 1936.

962   SANTOS, Egberto E. "The Bibliography of the Guitar," *Guitar News*
      (April-June, 1971): 14-15.

963   SCHEIT, Karl. "Von der Gitarre," *Musikerzeihung* V (1951): 21-23.

964   SCHIOZZI, B. "L'evoluzione della chitarra," *Musica Jazz* 19 (November,
      1963): 15-22.

965   SCHROEN, Egmont. *Die Gitarre und ihre Geschichte.* Leipzig, 1879.

966   SCHWARTZ-REIFLINGEN, E. "La chitarra in Germania," *La Chitarra*
      I (1934): 3ff.

SCHWEIZER, G. "Die Guitarre Maria Stuarts," *ZfM* 114 (1953):   **967**
409-10.

SICCA, Mario. "La chitarra e gli strumenti a tastiera," *IFr*   **968**
I (October, 1972): 27-30.

STEVENSON, Robert M. *Music in Aztec and Inca Territory*. Berkeley: **969**
University of California Press, 1968, pp. 234-35.

TAPPERT, W. "Zur Geschichte der Gitarre," *MfM* XIV (1882): 77-85.   **970**

TESSARECH, J. *Évolution de la guitare*. Paris: H. Lèmoîne, 1923.   **971**

————. "Évolution de la guitare," *Die Gitarre* XI/9-10 (1930).   **972**

TERZI, B. *Teoria e insegnamento de la chitarra: Appunti*. Bologna,   **973**
1935.

TURNBULL, Harvey. *The Guitar from the Renaissance to the*   **974**
Present Day. London: Batsford Ltd., 1974. 168p.

TYLER, James. "The Renaissance Guitar 1500-1650," *EM* III/4   **975**
(October, 1975): 341-47.

VALMAN, B. L. *Gitara i Gitaristy*. Leningrad: Muzyka, 1967. 188p.   **976**

VIGLIETTI, Cedar. *Origen e historia de la guitarra*. Buenos Aires,   **977**
Editorial Albatross, 1973. 289p.

VISSER, D. "De ontwikeling van het gitaarspel in Nederland,"   **978**
Mens en Melody 14 (1959): 183-86.

VOIGT, A. "Beiträge zur Geschichte der Gitarre," *ZfIb* 47 (1927):   **979**
19ff.

WADE, Graham. "An Historical Perspective of the Guitar Duo,"   **980**
GR 31 (1969): 7-8.

ZUTH, Josef. "Die englische und die deutsche Gitarre des   **981**
Ausgehenden 18. Jahrhunderts," *Die Gitarrefreund* 22/8
(1922).

982 ————. "Die Leipziger Allgemeine Musikalische Zeitung (1798-1848) als gitarristische Quelle," *Die Gitarre* I (1919-1920): 4-12; II (1920-1921): 1-2, 11-12.

983 ————. "Vom Leben und Sterben der Gitarre in Alt-Wien," *ZfdG* II (1922-1923) heft 5.

See also: 1, 9, 11, 12, 13, 63, 64, 83, 105, 106, 138, 139, 140, 141, 164, 182, 183, 184, 185, 186, 209, 210, 211, 212, 213, 214, 215, 282, 284, 289, 303, 352, 359, 366, 367, 372, 416, 425, 426, 430, 433, 442, 443, 459, 461, 468, 469, 470, 487, 488, 490, 491, 492, 493, 494, 497, 499, 544, 555, 580, 652, 686, 743, 758, 775, 986, 1004, 1017, 1037, 1038, 1052, 1053, 1057, 1077, 1084, 1088, 1121, 1122, 1123, 1125, 1128, 1136, 1137, 1203, 1214, 1422, 1446, 1450, 1474, 1479, 1650, 1653, 1684: pp. 157-218, 1699, 1706, 1707, 1713. Chilesotti, O. "La Chitarra francese: appunti," *RMI* XIV (1907); Schwartz-Reiflingen, E. "Zur Literatur der Gitarre," *Die Gitarre* IX (1928): 9-10.

ICONOGRAPHY / DESCRIPTION

984 Anon. "The Medieval, Renaissance and Baroque Lute," *EM* 3/2 (April, 1975): 137-39.

985 BAINES, Anthony. *Musical Instruments Throughout the Ages.* Baltimore: Penguin Books, 1961.

986 BOBRI, Vladimir. "A Gallery of Great Guitars from the XVI to the XX Century," *GR* 30 (1968): 13-27; 32 (1969): 15-31; 35 (1971): 9-27.

987 BONNER, Stephen. "Two Renaissance Lute Carvings," *LSJ* XIII (1971): 36-39.

988 DART, Thurston. "The Instruments in the Ashmolean Museum," *GSJ* VII (1954): 7-9.

989 DENIS, Valentin. "Musical Instruments in Fifteenth-Century Netherland and Italian Art," *GSJ* II (1949): 40-41.

990 ————. *De Muziekinstrumenten in de Nederlanden en in Italie naar hun Afbeelding in de 15e-eeuwsche Kunst.* Antwerpen: Uitgeversmij N.v. Standart-boekhandel, 1944. 531p.

FINLAY, Ian F. "Musical Instruments in 17th-Century Dutch   991
Paintings," *GSJ* VI (1953): 52-69.

GALPIN, Francis W. *Old English Instruments of Music.* Edited by   992
Thurston Dart. London: Methuen, 1966.

GEIRINGER, Karl. *Die Flankenwirbelinstrument in der bildender*   993
Kunst der Zeit zwischen 1300 und 1550. Unpublished Ph.D.
diss., Wien, 1923.

————. "Vorgeschichte und Geschichte der Europäischen Laute bis   994
zum Beginn der Neuzeit," *ZfMw* X (1927): 560-603.

HAHNE-OVERMANN, Elisabeth. "Ikonographie der Lautengriffe,"   995
ZfMw XII (1929): 527-30.

KINSKY, Georg. *A History of Music in Pictures.* New York: Dover,   996
1951, pp. 57, 67, 68, 70.

LEICHTENTRITT, H. "Was lehren uns die Bildwerke des 14.-17.   997
Jahrhunderts über die Instrumental-Musik ihrer Zeit?" *SIMG*
VII (1905-1906): 315-64.

LEPPERT, Richard D. *Musical Instruments and Performing Ensembles*   998
in Flemish Paintings in the Seventeenth Century. Unpublished
Ph.D. diss., Indiana University, 1973.

MACLEISH, Martin. "An Inventory of Musical Instruments at the   999
Royal Palace, Madrid, in 1602," *GSJ* 21 (1968): 108-28.

PRAETORIUS, Michael. *Syntagma Musicum.* Vol. 2: *De*   1000
Organographia, Wolfenbüttel 1619. Facsimile edition by W.
Gurlitt. Kassel: Bärenreiter Verlag, 1958.

SAFFLE, Michael. "Lutes and Related Instruments in Eight   1001
Important European and American Collections-part I," *JLSA*
VIII (1975): 22-48.

SPENCER, Robert. "How to Hold a Lute: Historical Evidence From   1002
Paintings," *EM* 3/4 (October, 1975): 352-54.

WANGERMÉE, Robert. *Flemish Music and Society in the Fifteenth and*   1003
Sixteenth Centuries. New York: Praeger, 1968, pp. 55, 63, 148, 165,
233.

Instrumentation

1004 WELLER, M. P. I. *Some Steps in the Evolution of the Spanish Guitar and Related Instruments, Based on a Consideration of Iconographic Evidence.* Newcastle (MLH) diss., forthcoming.

1005 WINTERNITZ, E. *Musical Instruments and Their Symbolism in Western Art.* New York: Norton, 1967. 240p.

1006 ———. "On Angel Concerts in the 15th Century," *MQ* XLIX (1963): 450-63.

See also: 1124.

INSTRUMENTATION

1007 BACHER, J. "Die Renaissance-Laute im Zusammenspiel mit Blockflöte und Gamben," *Zeitschrift für Hausmusik* VIII (1939): 53-59.

1008 BLOCH, S. "Music for the Lute and Recorder," *Musical America* 69 (April 15, 1959): 16.

1009 BOWLES, Edmund A. "Haut and Bas: The Grouping of Musical Instruments in the Middle Ages," *MD* VIII (1954): 115-40.

1010 ———. "Instruments at the Court of Burgundy (1363-1467)," *GSJ* 6 (1953): 41-51.

1011 BROWN, Howard M. *Sixteenth-Century Instrumentation: The Music of the Florentine Intermedii.* Musicological Studies and Documents, No. 30. New York: American Institute of Musicology, 1973. 229p.

1012 COHEN, Albert. "A Study of Instrumental Ensemble Practise in Seventeenth-Century France," *GSJ* XV (1962): 3-15.

1013 EDWARDS, Warwich A. "The Performance of Ensemble Music in Elizabethan England," *PRMA* 97 (1971): 113-23.

1014 EITNER, Robert. "Die Instrumental-begleitung der Italienische Musikdramen," *MfM* 27 (1895): 1-62.

1015 FORTUNE, Nigel. "Continuo Instruments in Italian Monodies," *GSJ* VI (1953): 10-14.

102

FOX, Charles W. "An Early Duet for Recorder and Lute," *GR* **1016**
9 (1949): 24-25.

GARNSEY, Sylvia. "The Use of Hand-Plucked Instruments in the **1017**
Continuo Body: Nicola Matteis," *M&L* 47 (1966): 35-40.

HAAS, R. "Die Verwendung der Lauteninstrumente in der Oper," **1018**
ZfdG IV/8-9 (1925).

JEFFERY, Brian. "Instrumentation in the Music of Antony Holborne," **1019**
GSJ XIX (1966): 20-26.

LaRUE, Jan. "Lute Music," *KONGRESS 1961*, pp. 73-75. **1020**

MOORE, Verna L. "Psalmes, Tears and Broken Music," *Bulletin of* **1021**
John Rylands Library (Manchester) (1964), pp. 411-28.

MORROW, M. and M. GRAUBORT (transl.) "Lutes and Theorboes: **1022**
Their Use as Continuo Instruments, Described by Praetorius in
His Syntagma Musicum, 1619," *LSJ* II (1960): 26-32.

THOMAS, Bernard. "The Renaissance Flute," *EM* (January, **1023**
1975): 9-10.

WEAVER, Robert L. "Sixteenth-Century Instrumentation," *MQ* **1024**
XLVII (1961): 363-77.

WILLETTS, P. "Autographs of Angelo Notari," *M&L* (1969), **1025**
pp. 124-26.

ZINGEL, H. J. "Zupfinstrumente des Continuo," *ZfMw* XVII **1026**
(1934), pp. 35, 306-307.

LUTE HISTORY / GENERAL

Anon. Kommision für Erforschung der Lautenmusik," *ZIMG* **1027**
14 (1912-1913): 1-8.

ALTOVITI AVILA, Angelina (Toscanelli). *Il Liuto: notize espliestivo e* **1028**
storiche di A. Toscanelli, . . . seguite da un cenno sul modo di leggere
l'intavolature del Prof. B. Landini. Milano: G. Podrocco, 1921. 80p.

1029 ANDERSON, Otto E. *Musik och Musikinstrument.* Bonnier, 1934.

1030 APEL, Willi. "Solo Instrumental Music," in *NOHM* vol. 4, pp. 682-704.

1031 BAINES, Anthony. "Fifteenth-Century Instuments in Tinctoris' 'De Inventione et Usu Musicae'," *GSJ* III (1950): 19-26.

1032 BARON, Ernst G. "Beiträge zur historische-theoretische und praktische Untersuchung der Laute," in Marburg's *Historische-Kritische Beiträge* vol. 2. Berlin: Lange, 1756, pp. 65-83.

1033 BECK, Sydney. "The Decline of the Lute," *GR* 9 (1949): 8-12.

1034 BEHN, F. "Die Laute im Altertum und frühen Mittlealter," *ZfMw* I (1918): 89-107.

1035 BERMUDO, Juan. *Comiencer el libro primero de la declaración de instrumentos.* Ossuna (de Leon) 1549. Facsimile edition, edited by S. M. Kastner. Kassel: Bärenreiter Verlag, 1975. 314p.

1036 BICKFORD, Vadah O. "When All the World Played Lutes," *Musical Observer* 30 (1931): 5-7, 25.

1037 BISCHOFF, H. "Eineges über Laute und Gitarre," *Zfm* (1939) 826ff.

1038 ———. "Laute und Gitarre," *Deutsche Tonkunstler Zeitung* 28 (1932): 6ff.

1039 BOETTICHER, Wolfgang. "Arbeitsgemeinschaft zum Studium der Lautenmusik," *KONGRESS 1958,* pp. 329-31.

1040 ———. "Laute," *MGG* 8:345-82.

1041 ———. *Studien zur soloistischen Laute-Praxis des 16. und 17. Jahrhunderts.* Unpublished Ph.D. diss., Berlin, 1943.

1042 ———. "Tagung zur Studium der Älteren Lautenpraxis," *Mf* 11 (1958): 214.

1043 BOSQUET, Emile. *La Musique de Clavier, et par extension de Luth. Manuel Encyclopedique Historique et Pratique.* Brussels, 1953.

BRANCOUR, René. "Le régne du luth," *Le Menestrel* 90 (1923): 37ff. **1044**

BRANZOLI, Giuseppi. *Ricerche sullo studio del liuto*. Roma: Loescer, **1045**
1889.

BRONDI, Maria R. *Il liuto e la chitarra, ricerche storiche sulla loro* **1046**
origine e sul loro sviluppo. Turin: Bocca, 1926. [Originally in
Rivista Musicale Italiano XXXII (1925): 1-39, 161-95, 317-62;
XXXIII (1926): 1-20, 181-209.]

BRUGER, H. D. "Die Laute in der Staatlische Privatmusiklehrerprüfung," **1047**
Deutsche Tonkunstler Zeitung 27 (1931): 497ff.

————. "Zur Literatur über alte Lautenmusik," *Die Laute* 4/5-6 **1048**
(1921).

CAMPBELL, Richard G. *Zur Typologie der schalenlanghalslaute.* **1049**
Ph.D. diss., Free University of Berlin, 1963; published Strasbourg/
Baden-Baden: Heitz, 1967. 138p.

CARLSSON, C. A. "Något om lutan," *Slöjd och Ton* (1933), **1050**
pp. 17-19.

CERETTO, Scipione. *Della prattica musica vocale et strumentale* **1051**
Neapel (Carlino) 1601, pp. 313-19.

CHARNASSÉ, Hélène. *Les Instruments à Cordes Pincés*. Paris: **1052**
Presses Universitaires de France, 1970. 126p.

CHIESA, Rugerro. "Storia della letteratura del liuto e della chitarra," **1053**
IFr I (October, 1972): 21-26, I/2 (1973): 11-15, I/3 (1973):
22-26, I/4 (1973): 20-25; III/10 (1975): 20-24.

CHILESOTTI, Oscar. *Lautenspieler des XVI Jahrhundert. Ein* **1054**
Beitrag zur Kenntnis des Ursprungs der Moderne Tonkunst.
Facsimile reprint of Leipzig edition (1891). Bologna: Arnaldo
Forni, Editore, n.d. 248p.

————. "Un po di musica passato," *RMI* XVIII (1912): 858-63. **1055**

————. Primo congresso liutai romagnoli in Lugo," *RMI* 22 (1915): **1056**
168-69.

1057 ———. *Studi sul liuto e la chitarra.* Facsimile reprint of the offprint from *Rivista Musicale Italiana.* Bologna: Forni, 1967. 180p.

1058 CHOTTIN, A. "Le luth et les harmonies de la nature," *RM* XXI (1940): 197-203.

1059 DANNER, Peter. "Before Petrucci: The Lute in the Fifteenth Century," *JLSA* V (1972): 4-17.

1060 DISERTORI, Benvenuto. "Le liuto soprano," in *Le Luth et sa Musique,* edited by J. Jacquot. Paris: CNRS, 1958, pp. 231-38.

1061 DODGE, Janet. "Lauten-Musik des 16. und 17. Jahrhunderts," *Der Gitarre Freund* 28 (1928) 1/2 and 7/8.

1062 ———. "Lute Music of the XVIth and XVIIth Centuries," *PRMA* XXXIV (1908): 123-51.

1063 DOLMETSCH, Arnold. "The Lute," *Connoisseur* (April-May, 1904), pp. 213-17, (June-July, 1904), pp. 23-28.

1064 DORFMÜLLER, Kurt. *Studien zur Lautenmusik in der ersten Hälfte des 16. Jahrhundert.* Ph.D. diss., Munich, 1952. Published as *Studien zur Lautenmusik des 16. Jahrhunderts.* Tutzing: Verlag Max Schneider, 1967. 205p.

1065 ECORCHEVILLE, Jules. "Commision internationale pour l'étude de la musique pour luth," *ZIMG* VIII (1906-1907): 460-61.

1066 ———. "Le luth et sa musique," *Bulletin de la société internationale de musicologie* IV (1908): 131ff.

1067 EINSTEIN, A. "Gambe und Laute," *Musik im Haus* VI/1 (1926).

1068 ENGEL, Egon. *Die Instrumentalformen in der Lautenmusik des 16. Jahrhunderts.* Unpublished Ph.D. diss., Berlin, 1915.

1069 ———. *Von den Anfängen der Lauten-Musik.* Berlin: Private publication, 1915.

1070 ———. "Zu neuen Lautenbewegung," *Die Gitarre* 9 no. 7-8 (1928).

FRIBERG, C. H. "Gamba och nya stränginstrument," *Slöjd och Ton*   **1071**
(1943), pp. 67-69.

GERWIG, Walter. "Ein Brief und die Lautenspieler," *Hausmusik*   **1072**
XIV (November-December, 1952): 170-71.

GILL, Donald. "Brief Notes on the Bass Lute," *LSJ* III (1961): 27ff.   **1073**

———. The Elizabethan Lute, *GSJ* XII (1959): 60-62.   **1074**

GODWIN, Jocelyn. "Instruments in Robert Fludd's Utriusque   **1075**
Cosmi . . . . Historia," *GSJ* XXVI (1973): 2-14.

———. "Robert Fludd on the Lute and Pandora," *LSJ* XV   **1076**
(1973): 11-19.

HARRIS, D. "Music for the Lute and Classic Guitar," *Music Journal*   **1077**
(Australia) (1969), pp. 48ff.

JACQUOT, Jean. "The International Cataloque of Music for the Lute   **1078**
and Kindred Instruments," *Hinrichsen's Music Book* 11
(1961): 214-17.

———. *Le Luth et sa Musique.* [Collection of Essays on the Lute,   **1079**
edited by J. Jacquot.] Paris: CNRS, 1958. 352p.

———. "Le luth et sa musique, vers une organisation internationale   **1080**
des recherches," *AMl* XXX (1958): 89-98.

———. "La musique pour luth," *KONGRESS 1961*, pp. 75-88.   **1081**

———. "Premières résultats acquis—perspectives d'avenir," in   **1082**
Le luth et sa musique. Paris: CNRS, 1958, pp. 311-42.

JOHNSON, M. and C. ARNOLD. *To Introduce the Lute and Its Family.*   **1083**
London, 1945.

KIRSCH, Dieter. "Laute und Gitarre," *Kontakte* 5 (1968): 167-72.   **1084**

KLIMA, Josef. "Laute und Lautenmusik in Europen," *ÖMZ*   **1085**
XVI (1961): 529-38.

1086 KOCZIRZ, Adolf. "Studien zur alten Lautenmusik," *Die Gitarre* III/8 (1922).

1087 KÖRTE, Oswald. *Laute und Lautenmusik bis zur Mitte des 16. Jahrhunderts.* Ph.D. diss., Leipzig, 1901. Published in *Beiheft IMG* III (1901).

1088 KOSACK, H. P. "Laute und Gitarre," *Die Gitarre* XII/3-6 (1930).

1089 LAADE, Wolfgang. "Vom Klingenden Stab zu Laute," *Kontakte* (1959), pp. 42-43.

1090 LAIBLE, F. "Laute und Lautenmusik im Jahre 1950," *Hausmusik* (September-October, 1950), pp. 125-28.

1091 ———. "Laute und Theorbe," *Die Gitarre* I/10 (1919).

1092 ———. "Um die Laute," *Der Gitarrefreund* 29/7-8 (1929).

1093 LANG, P. "Le luth," *RM* 27 (1928-1929): 150-66.

1094 LESURE, François. "Le traité des instruments de musique de Pierre Trichet," *AnnMl* IV (1956): 192-200, 208-23.

1095 LIESMANN, Erika. "Die Stössel-Laute," *Musikinstrument* XVIII/2 (1969): 164-66.

1096 LORAINE, Michael. "Description of a Lute," *JLSA* V (1972): 68-69.

1097 LOZZI, C. "Di alcune scoperte riguardanti la storia del liuto," *Bibliofilia* VI (1904-1905): 13ff.

1098 LUMSDEN, David. "Un catalogue internationale des sources de la musique pour le luth," in *Le luth et sa musique.* Edited by J. Jacquot. Paris: CNRS, 1958, pp. 297-302.

1099 MAGNI, Duflocq. *Storia del liuto.* Milan: Edizione Tito, 1931. 85p.

1100 MAIRY, Adrienne and L. de LA LAURENCIE. "Le luth," in *Encyclopédie de la musique.* Edited by Lavignac. Part I, vol. 8, pp. 1972-90.

MARTELL, P. "Zur Geschichte der Laute," *Die Harmonie* 13/10-11   **1101**
(1922).

————. "Zur Geschichte der Lauten," *Der Lauten-Spieler* 2/1+   **1102**
(1926): 1ff.

MERSENNE, Marin. *Harmonie Universelle (1636)*. Facsimile edition   **1103**
Paris: CNRS, 1963, vol. 3 [also transl. by R. Chapman. The
Hague: M. Nijhoff, 1957].

MÜLLER, Adolf. "Für die Berederung der Lautenmusik," *Die*   **1104**
Harmonie 10/5-6 (1918).

MÜLLER, Fritz. "Die Lauten und ihre Geschichte," *Deutsche Musik*   **1105**
Zeitung 57-58/18 (1925).

MÜLLER-BLATTAU, J. "Laute und Lautenmusik," *Mf* 13   **1106**
(1960): 191-94.

NOULET, F. "Notice sur le luth," *Mémoires de la société*   **1107**
archéologique de la Corrèze (1895), p. 58ff.

PANUM, Hortense. "Nordeuropas gamle Strenginstrumenter,"   **1108**
Forening til Norske fortidsmindesmaerkers bevaring (1903),
pp. 107-42.

PARIGI, A. "Il liuto accordato," *Musica d'oggi* XXI/12 (1939):   **1109**
363-67.

PARRINI, A. *Dalle ricerche sul liuto ad un sinfonista sconosciuto*   **1110**
del 1600. Florenze, 1925.

PICOLELLIS, G. de. *Liutai antichi e moderni*. Firenze, 1885.   **1111**
Facsimile reprint Kassel: Bärenreiter, n.d. 191p.

POULTON, Diana. "Notes on Some Differences Between the Lute   **1112**
and the Vihuela and Their Music," *Consort* 16 (July, 1959):
22-26.

PRYNNE, Michael W. "Lute," *Grove* 5:433-39.   **1113**

PULVER, J. "The Language of the Lutenist," *Sackbut* VI (1925-1926):   **1114**
333-36.

1115 REINHARDT, K. "Stufen der Lauten begleitung," *Die Laute* II 5/6 (1919).

1116 ROBERTS, J. D. "The Lute: Historical Notes," *LSJ* II (1960): 17-25.

1117 ROSKETH, Yvonne. "The Instrumental Music of the Middle Ages and the Early Sixteenth Century," in *NOHM*, pp. 440-43, 487-89, 489-91.

1118 ROTTMANN, K. "Kleine Erfahrung eines Lautenmeister," *Hausmusik* 21 (January-February, 1957): 18-20.

1119 RUTH-SOMMER, H. "Die Laute," *Die Musik* IV/3 (1904): 13-20.

1120 SAFFER, D. R. "Advice to the Lute-Lorn," *American Music Teacher* (February-March, 1969), p. 19.

1121 SAINZ de LA MAZA, Regino. *La musica de laud, vihuela y guitarra del Renascimento al Barroco*. Madrid: Real Academia de Bellas Artes de San Fernando, 1958. 43p.

1122 SCHWARTZ-REIFLINGEN, E. (ed.) *Laute-Almanach, ein Jahr- und Handbuch für alle Laute- und Gitarre-Spieler*. Berlin, 1919-1920.

1123 SOMMER, Hermann. "Die Darstellung der Laute in der Malerei und im Kupferstich," in *Laute-Almanach*. Edited by Schwartz-Reiflingen. Berlin, 1919, pp. 17-21.

1124 ———. *Die Laute in ihrer Musikgeschichtliches Kultur- und Kunsthistorische Bedeutung*. Berlin, 1920. 88p.

1125 *Laute und Gitarre*. Stuttgart: J. Engelhorn, 1922. 99p.

1126 SÖRNSEN, Nils. "Die dopple-chörige Laute," *Die Lautenspieler* II/3 (1926).

1127 ———. *Meine Laute, ein Buch aus der Erfahrung für Liebhaber und Freunde der Lautenmusik*. Stuttgart: Franckh'sche Verlagsbuchhandlung, 1924.

1128 STAINER, John F. R. "Lutes and Guitars," *MT* no. 678 (1899): 55ff.

STERNFELD, Frederik W. "Recent Research on Lute Music," *M&L*   1129
39 (1958): 139-42.

STEVENS, William F. *A Study of the Lute and Its Music to Accompany*   1130
a Master's Recital. Unpublished Master's thesis, San Jose State
University, 1973. 66p.

STRADNER, Gerhard. *Sebastian Virdungs Musica getutscht als*   1131
Quelle des Instrumentariums und der Spielpraxis im frühen
16. Jahrhunderts. Ph.D., Saarbrüchen, forthcoming.

SZCZEPANSKA, M. "Alte Meister der Laute," *Kwartalnik Muzyczny*   1132
IV (1928): 16ff.

TILMOUTH, M. "Some Improvements in Music Noted by William   1133
Turner in 1697," *GSJ* X (1958): 57-59. [Concerns
abandonment of plucked-string instruments].

TINTORI, Giampiero and Gianluigi DARDO. "Il Liuto," in   1134
Enciclopedia della Musica, vol. 3. Milan: G. Ricordi, 1964,
pp. 25-30.

TREML, R. "Lauten und Gitarre," *Collegium Musicum* I/5-6 (1933).   1135

————. "Laute- und Gitarre, die Spielpraxis," *Volkslied und*   1136
Hausmusik II (1935): 183ff.

WALDNER, F. "Zwei Inventarien aus dem 16. und 17. Jahrhundert,"   1137
SzMw IV (1916): 132-47.

WARD, John. "Le problème des hauters dans la musique pour luth   1138
et vihuela au XVIe siècle," in *Le luth et sa musique.* Edited by
J. Jacquot. Paris: CNRS, 1958, pp. 171-78.

WASIELEWSKI, Josef W. von. *Geschichte der Instrumentalmusik im*   1139
16. Jahrhundert. Berlin: Verlag Guttenberg, 1878, pp. 29-49,
109-18, 130-33.

WEINMANN, K. "Ein unbekannter Traktat des Johannes Tinctoris,"   1140
Festschrift REIMANN, pp. 267-71.

1141 WILKOWSKA-CHOMINSKA, Krystyna. "A la recherche de la musique pour luth," in *Le luth et sa musique*. Edited by J. Jacquot. Paris: CNRS, 1958, pp. 193-208.

See also: 1, 10, 11, 12, 13, 892, 906, 941, 942, 1684, 1731.

LUTE HISTORY / ENGLAND

1142 BUMTEN, A. Chambers. "Some Old Scottish Lute Music," *Scottish Musical Magazine* 3 (1922): 185-87.

1143 BYLER, Arthur. *Italian Currents in the Popular Music of England in the Sixteenth Century*. Unpublished Ph.D., University of Chicago, 1952. 206p.

1144 CHARTERIS, Richard. "Jacobean Musicians at Hatfield House, 1605-1613," *RMA* 12 (1974): 115-36.

1145 DIMSDALE, V. L. *The Lute in Consort in 17th-Century England*. Unpublished Ph.D., Oxford (LMH), 1968.

1146 DODGE, Janet. "Lutenists and Lute Music in England," *Euterpe* VII (1907): 34ff.

1147 FELLOWES, Edmund H. "The English Lutenists," *Sackbut* II (1922): 36ff.

1148 FINNEY, Gretchen. *Musical Backgrounds for English Literature: 1580-1650*. New Jersey: Rutgers University Press, 1961. 292p.

1149 FITZGIBBON, H. M. "Instruments and Their Music in the Elizabethan Drama," *MQ* XVII/3 (1931): 319-29.

1150 HARRIS, David G. T. "Musical Education in Tudor Times," *PRMA* 65 (1938-1939): 109-39.

1151 LEFKOWITZ, Murry. "The Longleat Papers of Bulstrode Whitlocke; New Light on Shirley's Triumph of Peace," *JAMS* 18 (1965): 42-60.

LONG, John. *Shakespeare's Use of Music: A Study of the Music and*   **1152**
Its Performance in the Original Production of Seven Comedies.
Gainsville: University of Florida Press, 1955. 213p.

LUMSDEN, David. "English Lute Music 1540-1620, an Introduction,"   **1153**
PRMA LXXXIII (1956-1957): 1-13.

————. "The Lute and Its English Music," *Listener* (1953), p. 578ff.   **1154**

————. "The Lute in England," *The Score* VIII (September, 1953):   **1155**
36-43.

————. "De quelques élèments étrangers dans la musique anglaise   **1156**
pour le luth," in *Le luth et sa musique*. Edited by J. Jacquot.
Paris: CNRS, 1955, pp. 197-204.

————. "The Sources of English Lute Music (1540-1620)," *GSJ*   **1157**
VI (1953): 14-22.

————. *The Sources of English Lute Music, 1540-1620.* Unpublished   **1158**
Ph.D. diss., Cambridge (England), 1955. 3 vols.

NAYLOR, Edward. *Shakespeare and Music.* Rev. ed. London: Dent   **1159**
and Sons, 1931. 212p.

NEWCOMB, Wilburn W. *Studien zur englischen Lautenpraxis im*   **1160**
elisabethanischen Zeitalter. Kassel: Bärenreiter, 1968. 135p.

NEWTON, Richard. "English Duets for Two Lutes," *LSJ* (1959):   **1161**
23-30.

————. "English Lute Music in the Golden Age," *PRMA* 65   **1162**
(1938-1939): 63-90.

————. "The Cambridge Consort Books," *JLSA* V (1972): 70-104.   **1163**

NORDSTROM, Lyle. "Two New English Lute Duets," *JLSA* VI   **1164**
(1973): 46-47.

NORLIND, Tobias. "English Music for the Lute in the Time of   **1165**
Shakespeare," *KONGRESS 1911*, p. 331.

1166   NYE, Nancy L. *The Song of the English Lutenists.* Master's thesis, Texas Christian University, 1950. 152p.

1167   OLSHAUSEN, Ulrich. *Das Lautenbegleitete Solo-Lied in England um 1600.* Ph.D. diss., published Kassel: Bärenreiter, 1963. 342p.

1168   PATTISON, Bruce. "A Note on the 16th-Century Lute Songs," *MT* 71 (1930): 796-98.

1169   ————. "Literature and Music in the Age of Shakespeare," *PRMA* (1934): 67-86.

1170   ————. *Music and Poetry of the English Renaissance.* London: Methuen, 1948.

1171   POPOVICI, Doru. *Muzica elisabethana.* Bucuresti: Uniunii Compozitorilor, 1972. 159p.

1172   PULVER, Jeffrey. *A Biographical Dictionary of Old English Music.* London: Kegan Paul, 1927. 537p.

1173   ————. "Music in England During the Commonwealth," *AMl* VI (1934): 169-81.

1174   REYNOLDS, N. "Music and the Faeries," *Music in Education* 35 (1971): 439-40, 540-41.

1175   ROBERTS, John. (transl.) "An Eighteenth-Century Amateur Lutenist," *LSJ* VIII (1966): 38-40.

1176   ROOLEY, Anthony and James TYLER. "The Lute Consort," *LSJ* XIV (1972): 13-24.

1177   ROSS, L. J. "Shakespeare's Dull Clown and Symbolic Music," *Shakespeare Quarterly* XVII (September, 1966): 107-28.

1178   RUBSAMEN, W. H. "Scottish and English Music of the Renaissance in a Newly-Discovered Manuscript," *Festschrift BESSELER,* pp. 259-84.

1178a   RUFF, Lillian and D. Arnold WILSON. "The Lute Song and Elizabethan Politics," *Past and Present* 44 (1969): 3-51.

————. "Allusion to the Essex Downfall in Lute Song Lyrics," *LSJ*   1179
XII (1970): 31-36.

SABOL, A. "New Documents on Shirley's Masque The Triumph of   1180
Piece," *M&L* XLVII (1966): 10-26.

SCHOLL, Evely H. *A Study of the English School of Lutenist Song-*   1181
Writers. Unpublished Ph.D. diss., University of Michigan,
Ann Arbor, 1935.

STERNFELD, F. W. *Music in Shakespearean Tragedy*. London: 1182
Routledge and Kegan Paul, 1963. 333p.

TILMOUTH. M. "The Royal Academies of 1695," *M&L* 38 (1957):   1183
327-34.

WOODFILL, Walter L. *Musicians in English Society from Elizabeth*   1184
to Charles I. New York: Da Capo Press, 1969. 372p.

See also: **1235, 1431, 1478, 1488, 1500, 1501, 1503;** La Fontaine, H. C. de.
The King's Musick. London: Novello, [1909]. 522p.

LUTE HISTORY / FRANCE

L'Ancienne France. Le Théatre et la Musique jusqu'en 1789. Paris: 1185
Librairie de Firmin Dodot et Cie, 1887. pp. 236-37.

ANTHONY, James. *French Baroque Music*. London: Batsford,   1186
1974. pp. 227-37.

BRENET, Michel. "Notes sur l'histoire du luth en France," *RMI*   1187
V (1898): 63ff., VI (1899): 1-44.

JACQUOT, Jean. "Luth et clavesin français vers 1650," *KONGRESS*   1188
1967, pp. 115-58.

LA LAURENCIE, Lionel de. "Essai de chronologie de quelques   1189
ouvrages de luth de l'école français du dix-septième siècle,"
Bulletin de la société francaise de musicologie [=*Revue de*
Musicologie] (December, 1919), pp. 227-32.

1190 ————. "Les femmes et le luth en France au XVIIe et XVIII siècles," *Le Correspondent* (May, 1925), pp. 443-51.

1191 LESURE, François. "Recherches sur les luthistes parisiens à l'époque de Louis XIII," in *Le Luth et sa musique.* Edited by J. Jacquot. Paris: CNRS, 1958, pp. 209-24.

1192 RAVE, Wallace J. *Some Manuscripts of French Lute Music 1630-1700: An Introductory Study.* Unpublished Ph.D. diss., University of Illinois, Urbana-Champaign, 1972. 443p.

1193 ROLLIN, Monique. "Apropos d'un manuscrit de luth écrit en Normandie," *Mélanges du 12e au 17e siècles. No. 83, La Musique et les musiciens en Normandie.* Rouen: Association d'étude Normandes. 1957, p. 11ff.

1194 RUBSAMEN, Walter H. "The Earliest French Lute Tablature," *JAMS* XXI/3 (1968): 287-99.

1195 TESSIER, André. "Quelques sources de l'école français de luth du XVIIe siècle," *KONGRESS 1930*, pp. 222-24.

See also: 1420, 1421, 1426, 1464, 1480. Bruger, H. D. "Alte Lautenmusik," *Simrock Jahrbuch* (1928), pp. 130-44.

LUTE HISTORY / GERMANY

1196 AERDE, Raymond J. J. van. *Musicalia; notes pour servir à l'histoire de la musique, du théatre et de la danse à Malines . . . .* Malines: H. Dierickx-Beke fils, 1921. 72p.

1197 AMOS, Charles. *Lute Practise and Lutenists in Germany Between 1500 and 1750.* Unpublished Ph.D. diss., University of Iowa, 1975. 292p.

1198 BARON, Ernst G. *Historisch-Theoretisch und Pratische Untersuchung des Lauteninstruments der Lauten.* Facsimile reprint of 1727 edition. Amsterdam, 1965.

1199 ————. *The Study of the Lute.* Translated by Douglas Alton Smith. Redondo Beach, California: Instrumenta Antiqua Publications, 1975.

DIECKMANN, Jenny. *Die in deutscher Lauten-Tabulaturen über-*
lieferten Tänze des 16. Jahrhunderts. Unpublished Ph.D. diss.,
Kassel, 1931.

1200

GOMBOSI, Otto. "Eine deutsche Lauten-Tabulatur," *Ungarische*
Jahrbücher [=Ural-Altaische Jahrbücher] III (1923): 402-406.

1201

KLIMA, Josef. "Lauten tabulaturen in Niederösterreich,"
Niederösterreich I (1958).

1202

KOCZIRZ, Adolf. "Die Alt-Wiener Gitarre um 1800," *Österreich* I
(1925) no. 3, 1ff., no. 4, 2ff., no. 5, 2ff.

1203

————. "Böhmischen Lautenkunst um 1720," *Alt-Prager Almanach*
(1926), p. 88ff.

1204

————. "Lauten-Musik und Österreiche Lauten-Spieler bis 1750,"
ZIMG VI (1904-1905): 489.

1205

————. "Österreichische Lautenmusik zwischen 1650-1720,"
STMw V (1918): 1ff.

1206

————. "Ostpreussicher Lauten-Meister des 16. Jahrhunderts,"
Königsberger Hartung'sche Zeitung, (November 15, 1931).

1207

KOSACK, H-P. *Geschichte der Laute und Lautenmusik in*
Preussen. Ph.D. diss., Königsberg, 1933. Published Kassel:
Bärenreiter Verlag, 1935.

1208

————. "Die Lauten-Tabulaturen in Stammbuch des Burggrafen
Achatius zu Dohna," *Altpreussiche Beiträge* (1939).

1209

LAYER, Adolf. "Musik und Musiker der Fuggerzeit," in *Begleitheft*
zur Austellung der Stadt Augsburg, 1959.

1210

————. "Paduaner Lauten und ihre Schwäbischen Meister,"
Schwaben IX (1959): 175ff.

1211

LEEB, Hermann. "Die Laute des 16. Jahrhunderts," paper read
at the Bern/Solothurn/Freiburg chapter meeting of the
Schweitzerische Musik-forschenden Gesellschaft, 1948.

1212

1213 MALACEK, Anton. "Beiträge zur Geschichte der Wiener Lautenspieler," in *Jahrbuch des Vereins für Geschichte der Stadt Wien*. Vol. 13, 1957. 114ff.

1214 SCHEIT, Karl. "Gitarre und Laute in der Österreichischen Musik," *ÖMZ* 13 (1958): 191-95.

1215 SENN, W. *Musik und Theater am Hof zu Innsbruck*. Innsbruck: Österreichische Verlagsanstalt, 1954. 8, pp. 150-153, 334-35.

1216 TICHOTA, Jiri. "Deutsche Lieder in Prager Lautentabulaturen des Beginnenden 17. Jahrhunderts," *Miscellanea Musicologica* XX (1967): 66-69.

See also: **538, 713, 1220, 1502.**

LUTE HISTORY / ITALY

1217 ALMANSI, Carla. *I maestri liutai de Cremona. Realta e leggender di un'arte che non deve scomparire*. Cremona: Camera di Commercio, Industria e Agricoltura di Cremona, 1958. 14p.

1218 BERTOLOTTI, Angelo. *Musici alla corte dei Gonzaga in Mantova, dal secolo XV al XVIII*. Bologna: Editore Forni, 1969. 130p.

1219 BRESC, G. "Il liuto e la spada: un "Trovatore" in Sicilia nel Trecento," *Rivista de Musicologica* IX (1974): 37-47.

1220 CERVELI, Luisa. "Brevi note siu liutai tedeschi attivi in Italia dal secolo 16° al 18°," *Analecta Musicologica* V (1968): 299-337.

1221 DISERTORI, Benvenuto. "La leutista di Brere o del sonare a libro," *RMI* 43/6 (1939): 640-44.

1222 ———. "Remarque sur l'évolution du luth en Italia au XVe siècle et au XVIe," in *Le luth et sa musique*. Edited by J. Jacquot. Paris: CNRS, 1958, pp. 19-24.

1223 FRATI, Ludovico. "Liutisti e liutai di bolognesi," *RMI* (1919), pp. 94-111.

118

GABRIELLI, R. "I Liutai Ascolani," *RMI* 35 (1928):136.   **1224**

————. *I liutai Marchigiani: contributo all storia liutistica italiana.*   **1225**
Rome, 1935.

JAHIER, Enrico. "Liutisti italiani des renascimento, con saggi di   **1226**
interpretazione elettronica," in *Accademia toscana di scienze
e lettere "La Colombaria" atti e memorie.* (Firenze) 23
(1958-1959):171-205.

LEFKOFF, Gerald. *Five Sixteenth Century Venetian Lute Books.*   **1227**
Ph.D. diss., Catholic University of America, 1960. Pub.
Washington, D.C.: Catholic University of America, 1960.

MIXTER, Keith E. *Two Italian Lute Tablatures of 1536.* Unpublished   **1228**
Ph.D. diss., University of Chicago, 1941.

SELFRIDGE-FIELD, Eleanor. *Venetian Instrumental Music from*   **1229**
Gabrieli to Vivaldi. New York: Praeger, 1975, pp. 49-55,
69-77, 297-308.

VATIELLI, F. "Rapporti della musica violinisticacion l'ultima   **1230**
litteratura per liuto," *KONGRESS 1937*, pp. 292-98.

See also: 1245, 1424, 1435, 1438, 1442, 1451, 1453, 1466, 1474, 1483.

LUTE HISTORY / LOW COUNTRIES

LENAERTS, Rene B. "Improvisation auf der Orgel und Laute in den   **1231**
Niederlanden (16. und 17. Jahrhunderts)," *KONGRESS 1958*,
pp. 177-79.

————. "Nederlandse luittabulaturen uit de zestiende eeuw,"   **1232**
Vereniging voor Musiek-geschiedenis, Jaarboek, 1959, pp. 82-91.

NOSKE, Frits. "Early Sources of the Dutch National Anthem   **1233**
(1574-1626)," *Festschrift FEDOROV*, pp. 87-94.

————. "Remarques sur les luthistes des Pays-Bas, 1580-1620," in   **1234**
Le luth et sa musique. Edited by J. Jacquot. Paris: CNRS,
1958, pp. 179-92.

1235   RASCH, Rudi. "Seventeenth-Century Dutch Editions of English Instrumental Music," *M&L* 53/3 (1973):270-73.

1236   VAN DEN BORREN, Charles. *Les musiciens belges en Angleterre à l'époque de la Renaissance.* Brussel: Libraria des Deux Mondes, 1913, pp. 40-55.

1237   VAN DER STRAETEN, Edmund. *Musique aux Pays-Bas avant le 19e siècle*, vol. 1. Brussel, 1867, pp. 352-76, 377-404.

LUTE HISTORY / POLAND

1238   LISSA, Zofia. "La formation de style national dans la musique instrumentale Polonaise de la Renaissance," in *La musique instrumentale de la Renaissance.* Edited by J. Jacquot. Paris: CNRS, 1955, pp. 157-59.

1239   OPIENSKI, Henryk. *La musique Polonaise.* Paris: G. Cres, 1918, pp. 47-50.

1240   PANUFNIK, T. *Sztuka lutnicza studja nas budowa instrumentów smyczkowych.* Warsaw, 1926. 179p.

1241   POHANKA, Jaroslav. "O nejstaršich českých skladbách pro loutnu," *Hudebni Rozhledy* VIII (1955):245-46.

1242   RAMERTÓWNA, M. *Przyczynek do historii polskiej muzyki lutniowej w XVII wieku.* Unpublished Ph.D. diss., Lemberg, 1938.

1243   SIMPSON, Adrienne. "The Lute in the Czech Lands, An Historical Survey," *JLSA* IV (1971):9-20.

1244   STESZEWSKA, Z. (ed.) *Tance Polskie z Tablatur Lutniowych*, vol. 2. Cracow, 1966. See especially introduction.

1245   ————. "Tance włoskie w Polsce i Tance Polskie we Włoszech w XVI-XVII w.," [Italian dances in Poland and Polish dances in Italy in the 16th and 17th Centuries] *Muzyka* 56/1 (1970):15-30.

1246   SZCZEPANSKA, Maria. "Nieznana Krakowska tabulatura lutniowa z drugiej polowy XVI stulecia," *Festschrift CHYBYNSKI*, pp. 198-215.

TICHOTA, Jiri. "Die Aria Tempore Adventus Prodiecenda . . .   **1247**
ein beitrag zum stadium des Lautenspiels in Böhmen,"
Miscellenae Musicologica XXI-XXIII (1970): 153-70.

VOGL, Emil. "Lautenisten der böhmischen Spätrenaissance," *Mf*   **1248**
XVIII (1965): 281-90.

————. "Loutnová Hudba v Cechách," *Casopis Naródniho Musea*   **1249**
CXXXII/1 (1964): 11-20.

WILKOWSKA-CHOMINSKA, K. "Badania nad muzyka lutniowa w   **1250**
Polsce," *Muzyka* (1957), no. 3, pp. 18-36.

See also: **1436, 1439, 1440.**

LUTE HISTORY / SPAIN

APEL, Willi. "Early Spanish Music for Lute and Keyboard-   **1251**
Instruments," *MQ* XX (1934): 289-301.

MITJANA, Rafael. "La musique en Espagne," in *Encyclopédie de*   **1252**
la musique et Dictionaire du Conservatoire, part 1, vol. 4,
pp. 2017-25.

WARD, John. "The Lute in 16th-Century Spain," *GR* 9 (1949):   **1253**
27-28.

LUTE HISTORY / SCANDINAVIA

NOREN, A. and H. SCHÜCK. "Pär Brahes Visbok," *Svenska*   **1254**
Landsmålen och Svenskt Folklif II/4 (1894).

NORLIND, Tobias. "Den Svenska Lutan," *STfM* XVII (1935):   **1255**
5-43.

VRETBLAD, Åke. Något om Musikaliska Ornament i Svensk   **1256**
1700-Talspraxis," *STfM* 31 (1949): 155-60.

LUTE INSTRUCTION / METHODS

1257 AARVIG, C. A. *Luth-og Guitarspil, dets udvikling samt Tabulatur.* Kopenhagen: W. Hansen, 1930.

1258 BERNAU, Wilhelm. *Lautenschule; Anleitung zur schnellen und gründlichen Erlernung des Lauten- und Gitarrenspiels. . . .* Elberfeld: Verlag des Evangelischen Sängerbundes, E. V. 1932. 30p.

1259 BINKLEY, Thomas E. "Le luth et sa technique," in *Le luth et sa musique.* Edited by J. Jacquot. Paris: CNRS, 1958, pp. 25-36.

1260 BLACKMAN, Martha. "A Translation of Hans Judenkünig's 'Ain Schone Kunstlische Underweisung . . . (1523)'," *LSJ* XIV (1972): 29-42.

1261 BRANZOLI, Giuseppi. *Sunto Storico dell'Intavolatura.* Firenze: Venturi, 1891. 55p.

1262 BUETENS, Stanley. "Left-Hand Fingering of Difficult Single-Line Passages," *JLSA* IV (1971): 50-55.

1263 CASEY, William S. *Printed English Lute Instruction Books, 1568-1610.* Unpublished Ph.D. diss., University of Michigan, 1960, 2 vols. UM 60-02514.

1264 COLLES, H. C. "Some Musical Instruction Books of the 17th Century," *PRMA* (1928-1929), pp. 31-50.

1265 COX, Paul. *The Development of Classic Guitar Techniques as Reflected in Methods and Tutors of ca. 1780-1850.* Ph.D. diss., University of Indiana, forthcoming.

1266 CRASHAW, R. "Stuart Lute Technique," *LSJ* VI (1964): 13.

1267 DART, Thurston. "La Méthode de Luth de Miss Mary Burwell," in *Le luth et sa musique.* Edited by J. Jacquot. Paris: CNRS, 1958, pp. 121-26.

1268 ———. "Miss Mary Burwell's Instruction Book for the Lute," *GSJ* XI (1958): 3-62.

ESCUDERO, J. C. "La méthode pour la guitar de Luis Briceño," **1269**
RMl LI (1965): 131-48.

GARROS, M. "L'art d'accompagnar sur la B. C. d'après G. G. **1270**
Nivers," *Festschrift MASSON*, pp. 45-51.

GERHARTZ, Karl. "Neue Wege und Ziele in der Plege der Lauten- **1271**
Musik," *ZfMw* 8 (1925-1926): 419-24.

GERWIG, Walter. "Das Spiel der Lauteninstruments," *Hausmusik* **1272**
17 (May-April, 1953): 37-42.

————. . . . *Wie begleite ich Volks- und Kinderlieder auf der Laute?* **1273**
Ein Weg zur Inprovisation eines Lautensatzes. Dresden: W.
Limpert, [1932]. 66p.

GIESBERT, F. J. *Schule für die Barocklaute*. Schott, 1939-1940. **1274**
117p.

HEARTZ, Daniel. "An Elizabethan Tutor for the Guitar," *GSJ* **1275**
16 (1973): 3-21.

————. "Les premières instructions pour le luth jusque ver 1550," **1276**
in *Le luth et sa musique*. Edited by J. Jacquot. Paris: CNRS,
1958, pp. 77-92.

————. "Les styles instrumentaux dens la musique de la **1277**
Renaissance," in *La musique instrumentale de la Renaissance*.
Edited by J. Jacquot. Paris: CNRS, 1955, pp. 61-76.

HENNING, Uta "The Lute Made Easy: A Chapter from Virdung's **1278**
Musica Getutscht (1515)," *LSJ* XV (1973): 20-36.

HUGHES, C. W. "An Elizabethan Self-Instruction for the Lute," **1279**
GR IX (1949): 29-30.

KOCZIRZ, Adolf. "Eine Title-Auflage Esajas Reusner (Erfreulich **1280**
Lautenkunst, 1697)," *ZfMw* (1925-1926): 636-40.

————. "Über die Figernageltechnik bei Saiteninstrumente," **1281**
Festschrift ADLER, pp. 164-67.

1282   LUECHTEFELD, Michael. *Some Relationships Between Musical Style and the Playing Technique of the Late Renaissance and Baroque Lutes.* Unpublished Master's thesis, Washington University, 1975.

1283   MOLZBERGER, Ernst. "Von der Fingerordnung (Applikation) beim Lauten- und Gitarrespiel," *Zeitschrift für Hausmusik* VIII/6 (1939): 185-87; IX/4 (1940): 75-78.

1284   ———. "Was bedeuten die ersten deutschen Lautenschule des 16. Jahrhunderts für die Lauten-Bewegung der Gegenwart," *Zeitschrift für Hausmusik* VI (1937-1938): 147-50.

1285   MURPHY, Sylvia. "Seventeenth-Century Guitar Music: Notes on Rasgeado Performance," *GSJ* XXI (1968): 24-32.

1286   MYERS, Joan. "Performance Practise Indications in Emanuel Adriansen's Lute Ensemble Music," *JLSA* II (1969): 18-27.

1287   NEEMANN, Hans. "Alte Lautenschulen," *Die Gitarre* VII (1926): 8ff.

1288   ———. "Lautenmusik-Neuausgaben in ihrer Bezeihung zur Notation und Spieltechnik," *AfMw* V (1940).

1289   ———. "Neue Wege zur Alten Lautenmusik," *Die Gitarre* VIII (1927).

1290   ———. "Die Spieltechnik der Alten Lauten Meister," *Die Gitarre* VI (1924-1925): 21ff.

1291   ———. "Vor der alten Laute und ihrem Spiel," *Deutsche Musikkultur* I (1936): 147-58.

1292   NEVEN, A. *Morphologie et technique de luth aux XVe et XVIe siècles.* Unpublished Ph.D. diss., n. p., n. d. [copy in University Library, Liège].

1293   POULTON, Diana. *An Introduction to Lute Playing.* London: Schott, 1961.

1294   ———. "How to Play with Good Style by Tomas de Santa Maria," *LSJ* XII (1970): 23-30.

1295   ———. "Notes on the Technique of the Lute," *MMR* 86 (1956): 4-7.

124

————. "Some Changes in the Technique of Lute Playing from 1296
LeRoy to Mace," *LSJ* I (1959): 7-18.

————. "La Technique de jeu du luth en France et en Angleterre," 1297
in *Le luth et sa musique*. Edited by J. Jacquot. Paris: CNRS,
1958, pp. 107-20.

SCHEIT, Karl. "Ce que nous enseignent les traités de luth des 1298
environs de 1600," in *Le luth et sa musique*. Edited by J. Jacquot.
Paris: CNRS, 1958, pp. 93-106.

SCHMID-KAYSER, Hans. *Kleine Lautenschule Erlernung der Laute-* 1299
und Gitarre-spiels nach Noten. Magdeburg: Heinrichhofen's
Verlag, [1937]. 23p.

SCHUBIGER, P. A. "System der Lauten [1532]," *MfM* VIII 1300
(1876): 6-7.

SCHWARTZ-REIFLINGEN, E. "Die Grundlagen des modernen 1301
Gitarre- und Lautenunterrichts," *Die Gitarre* 3/6 (1923).

SICCA, Mario. "Il vibrato come arriechimento naturale del suono. 1302
Suo studio sistematica sulla chitarra e sul liuto," *IFr* I/5 (1973):
24-26.

SMITH, Douglas Alton. "The Instructions in Matthaeus Waissel's 1303
Lautenbuch," *JLSA* VIII (1975): 49-79.

SOMMER, Hans. *Das Unterrichtswesen in den Lauten-Trakaten* 1304
des 16. unf 17. Jahrhundert. Unpublished Ph.D. diss., Berlin,
1922.

SUTTON, Julia. "The Lute Instruction of Jean-Baptiste Besard," 1305
MQ LI (1965): 345-62.

TONAZZI, Bruno. "L'arte di suonare la chitarra o cetre di Francesco 1306
Geminiani," *IFr* I (October, 1973): 13-20.

WEIGAND, George A. *Renaissance Instruction Books for Stringed* 1307
Instruments. Unpublished Master's thesis, University of
London, 1973.

1308 WOBERSIN, Wilhelm. *Schule für die Laute oder Bass-Gitarre nach neuen* .... Leipzig: Zimmerman, 1911. 2 vols. in 1.

1309 WÖLKI, Konrad. *Mandolone, Gitarre, Laute; eine Instrumentationslehre für Zupfinstrumente,* .... Berlin: H. Ragotzky, 1936. 32p.

1310 ZUTH, Josef. *Vorschule des Gitarren- und Lauten-Spiels.* Wien, 1919.

See also: 328: pp. 78-82, 84-89; 348, 349, 565, 607, 608, 631, 632, 931, 1197, 1198, 1199.

LUTHIERS

1311 Anon. "Polish Instruments and Constructors of Instruments in Poland," *Hinrichsen's Musical Year Book* VII (1952): 220-26.

1312 AERDE, Raymond van. "Les Tuerlinckx luthiers à Malines," *Koninklijke Kreng voor Oudheid-Kunde, Letteren en Kunst van Mechelin* [=*Cercle royal archéologique litteraire et artistique de Malines*]. 73 (1913): 13-210.

1313 BLÜMML, Emil. "Beiträge zur Geschichte der Lautenmacher in Wien," *ZfMw* II (1919-1920): 287-99.

1314 ———. "Der Wiener Geigen- und Gitarrenmacher Johann Georg Staufer," *ZfdG* III/1, 5 (1924).

1315 BOETTICHER, Wolfgang. "Gerle, Conrad," *MGG* 4: 1802-1804.

1316 BOIVIE, H. "Några Svenska lut- och fiolmakare unter 1700-talet," *Slöjd och Ton* (1942), pp. 1-3, 22-25.

1317 COUTAGNE, J. P. Henri. *Gaspard Duiffoproucart et les luthiers Lyonnais du XVIe siècle.* Paris: Librairie Fischbacher, 1893. 79p.

1318 CUCUEL, Georges. "Notes sur quelques musiciens, luthiers, éditeurs et graveurs de musique au XVIIIe siècle," *SIMG* 14 (1912-1913): 243-52.

1319 ENGEL, Egon. "Maler und Laute," *Die Gitarre* III/12 (1922).

FISORE, R. *Traité de lutherie ancienne*. Paris: Dupond, 1900. **1320**

GIRALDI, Romolo. "La liuteria italiana come arte populare," **1321**
Congresso nazionale di arte e tradizione populari (Firenze) no. 3
(1936): 350-51.

GUGGEMOS, G. "Die Tieffenbrucker von Tiefenbruck in Alt- Fussen," **1322**
Füssener Blatt no. 10 (1958): 83ff.; no. 1 (1959): 28ff.

HELLWIG, Günther. "Joachim Tielke," *GSJ* XVII (1964): 28-38. **1323**

HELLWIG, F. "Maker's Marks on Plucked Instruments of the 16th **1324**
and 17th Centuries," *GSJ* (1971): 22-32.

HERBECK, J. "Ein berühmter Lautenmacher und Geigenmacher. **1325**
Ein Biographie von Gaspar Tieffenbrucker," *Historische
Politische Blätter* (1909).

HOMOLKA, Ed. Em. Biographische Nachrichten über Lauten- und **1326**
Geigenmacher in Prag und Umgebung von der ältesten bis zur
unsere Zeit (1571-1900). *Zeitschrift für Instrumentenbau*
(October 11, 1901).

JACQUOT, Albert. *La lutherie lorraine et française depuis ses* **1327**
origines jusqu'a nos jours d'après les archives locales. Paris:
Fischbacher, 1912.

KINSKI, G. "Beiträge zur Tielke-Forschung," *ZfMw* IV (1923): **1328**
604-12.

―――. "Der Lautenmacher Hans Frei," *AMl* IX/1-2 (1937): 59-60. **1329**

LAYER, Adolf. *Das Allgäu–die Wiege der Lauten- und* **1330**
Geigenbaukunst. Feldafing/Obb.: Brehn, 1967. 17p.

―――. *Die Füssener Lautenmacherzunft Mattias Klotz von* **1331**
Mittenwald. Feldafing, 1959.

―――. "Kaspar Tieffenbrucker," *Lebensbilder aus dem* **1332**
Bayrischen Schwaben IV (1955).

LÜTGENDORFF, W. "Füssen die Wiege des Lauten- und **1333**
Geigenbaus," *Musik Industrie* II/9 (1922).

Luthiers

1334 ———. "Die Wiener Geigen- und Lautenmacher im 17. und 18. Jahrhunderts," *Neue Freie Presse* (Wien) Nr. 14408 (October 4, 1904).

1335 MALACEK, Anton. "Beiträge zur Geschichte der Wiener Lautenmacher in Mittlealter," in *Jahrbuch*, Verien für Geschichte der Staat Wien (1946-1947) fasc. 5/6, pp. 5-23. [Also printed separately, 23p.]

1336 MILLIOT, Sylvette. *Documents inédits sur les luthiers parisiens du XVIIIe siècle*. [1725-1800]. Ph.D. diss., University of Paris, 1970. Published—Paris: Société de française de musicologie, 1970. 241p.

1337 NIRRNHEIM, H. "Tielke—Hamburgische instrumentenbauer, insbesondere Geigen- und Lautenmacher," *Mitteilungen des Vereins für Hamburgische Geschichte* XIX (1898-1899):129-241.

1338 PERSYN, J. *Paul Kaul et la renaissance de la lutherie*. Leiden, 1934.

1339 PRYNNE, Michael. "A Note on Max Unverdorben," *LSJ* I (1959):58ff.

1340 ———. "The Old Bologna Lute Makers," *LSJ* V (1963):18-31.

1341 RIVET, Georges. "La Lutherie à Mirecourt," *Annales de L'Est* IV ser. 4 (1936):285-305.

1342 SCHERRER, Heinrich. *Der Lautenmacher. Eine Verlorengegangene Kunst von H. Scherrer, bayrischer kammervirtuos*. Leipzig: F. Hofmeister, 1920.

1343 SCHWARTZ-REIFLINGEN, E. "Zur Geschichte des Gitarrenbaus," *Der Gitarrefreund* 27/9-10 (1927).

1344 SJÖSTRAND, J. "Berömda lutbyggare i det gamla Stockholm," *Slöjd och Ton* (1931), pp. 18ff., 49ff., (1945), p. 37ff.

1345 STROCCHI, G. *Liuteria, storia ed arte*. Lugo: Instituto musicali, liutai e musicisti, 1937. 594p.

1346 SZULC, Z. "Lutnicy polscy od XVI wieku do czasów najnowszych oraz ich karteczki rozpoznaweze," [Polish lutenists from the 16th Century to the Present] *Festschrift Chybynski*, pp. 354-79.

1347 VIDAL, A. *La lutherie et les luthistes*. Paris, 1889.

WALDNER, F. *Nachrichten über tirolische Lauten- und Geigenbauer.* **1348**
Innsbruck, 1911. [Originally in *Ferdinadeum Zeitschrift* III
fasc. 55 (1911).]

See also: **20, 1191;** Mailand, Eugene. *Decouvert des anciens vernis italien
employes pour les instruments a cordes et a archet.* Paris,
1859; Savart, F. *Mémoire sur la construction des instruments
à cordes et à archet.* Paris, 1818; Starcke, Hermann. *Die
Geige, und Meister der Geigen- und Lautenbaukunst.* Dresden,
1884.

MANUSCRIPTS

AUSTRIA
Kremsmünster

FLOTZINGER, Rudolf. *Die Lautentabulaturen des Stiftes* **1349**
*Kremsmünster mit musikgeschichtlichen Ausweitung der
Handschriftlichen L64 und L81 sowie Thematischen Katalog
des Gesamtbestandes.* Ph.D. diss., Wien, 1964. Published in
series *Tabulae Musicae Austriacae.* Vienna: Bohlaus, 1965.

L79. See: **1192: pp. 359-62.**

L81. See: **375, 1192: pp. 118-23.**

Wien

HAAS, R. "Die Tabulaturbücher für Laute und Gitarre in der **1350**
Nationalbibliothek in Wien," *ZfdG* 5/2 (1926).

KLIMA, Josef. *Archiv alter Lautenmusik.* Marie Enzersdorf, **1351**
Kirchenstr. 23. Dr. Josef Klima (1957) typescript. 11p.

KOCZIRZ, Adolf. "Eine Gitarretabulaturen des Kais. Theorbisten **1352**
O. Cleminti," *Festschrift LA LAURENCIE*, pp. 107-15.

———. "Wiener Gitarre-Handschrifter von M. Giuliani," *Musik im* **1353**
Haus VI/1 (1927): 5ff. [=*Zeitschrift für die Gitarre*]

Manuscripts

1354 MAIER, Elisabeth. *Die handschriftlich überlieferten Tabulaturen für Lauteninstrument des 17. und 18. Jahrhunderts aus dem Bestand der Österreichischen Nationalbibliothek mit dem Wiener Luatenbuch des Jacques de Saint Luc.* Ph.D. diss., Wien, 1972.

1355 OREL, A. "Gitarremusik in der Wiener Stadtibibliothe," *ZfdG* 1/4 (1922).

1356 SZMOLYAN, Walter. "Das Archiv für alte Lautenmusik in Maria Enzersdorf bei Wien," *ÖMZ* XVI (1961): 538-44.

1357 ZUTH, Josef. "Die Mandolinhandschriften in der Bibliothek der Gesellschaft der Musikfreunde in Wien," *ZfMw* (1931-1932): 89-99.

Nationalbibliothek MS 17706. See: **1192: pp. 354-59.**

Gesellschaft der Musikfreunde MS 7763/92 (Schwanberg MS) *See:* **1192: pp. 383-87.**

BELGIUM

Bibliotheque du Conservatoire Royale de Musique MS Fa VI 10. See: **1192: pp. 180-83.**

BRITISH ISLES
England

Bedford County Record Office MS D.D. Tw. 7/2. See: **14.**

British Museum [British Library]

1358 BLOCH. S. "A Remarkable Elizabethan Lute Manuscript in the British Museum," *GR* 15 (1953): 9ff.

1359 HUGHES-HUGHES, Augustus. *Catalogue of Manuscript Music in the British Museum.* Vol. 3, London, 1906-1909, pp. 57-76.

1360 NOBLE, Jeremy. "Le Répertoire Instrumental Anglais: 1550-1585," in *La musique instrumentale de la Renaissance.* Edited by J. Jacquot. Paris: CNRS, 1955, pp. 91-114.

130

POULTON, Diana and David MITCHELL. "List of Printed Lute   **1361**
Music in the British Museum: Part I," *LSJ* XIII (1971):40-49.

————. "A List of Printed Lute Music in the British Museum: **1362**
Part II," *LSJ* XIV (1972):42-50.

WARD, John. "The Lute Music of MS Royal Appendix 58," *JAMS*   **1363**
XIII (1960):117-25.

  BM Stowe MS 389 (Ralph Bowles MS). *See:* **14.**

  BM MS Egerton 2046 (Jane Pickering). *See:* **1192: pp. 145-48.**

  BM MS Sloane 2923. See: **1192: pp. 350-54.**

  BM MS 2089. See: **1360.**

  BM add. MS 4900. See: **1360.**

  BM add. MS 16889. See: **1192: pp. 161-63.**

  BM add. MS 29246. See: **1360.**

  BM add. MS 29247. See: **1360.**

  BM add. MS 29396. See: **439.**

  BM add. MS 30513. See: **14, 1360.**

  BM add MS 31432. See: **438.**

Cambridge

HARWOOD, Ian. "The Origins of the Cambridge Lute Manuscripts,"   **1364**
LSJ V (1963):32-48.

MATHEW, A. G. "An Old Lute Book [Lowther LB]," *MT* 90   **1365**
(1949):189-91.

  MS Dd.2.11. See: **1444.**

  MS Dd. 4.23. See: **506.**

See also: 1163.

Manuscripts

London

1366 POULTON, Diana. "Checklist of Recently Discovered English Lute Manuscripts [Sampson LB; Board LB; Trumbull add. MS .6; Robarts LB; Mynshall LB; Burwell LB]," *EM* 3/2 (1975): 124-25.

1367 SPENCER, Robert. "Three English Lute Manuscripts [Mynshall LB; Sampson LB; Board LB]," *EM* 3/2 (1975): 119-24.

1368 ————. "The Tollemache [=Sampson LB] Lute Manuscript," *LSJ* VII (1965): 38-39.

London, Lambeth Palace

Lambeth Palace MS 1041. See: **1694.**

Oxford, Bodleian Library

1369 CUTTS, John P. "A Bodleian Song-Book: Don. c. 57.," *M&L* 34 (1954): 197ff.

Bodleian MS mus. b.1. See: **723, 725.**

Bodleian MS mus. Sch. f. 576. See: **1192: pp. 270-75.**

Bodleian MS mus. Sch. G 616. See: **1192: pp. 293-98.**

Bodleian MS mus. Sch. G 617. See: **1192: pp. 298-302.**

Bodleian MS mus. Sch. G 618. See: **1192: pp. 302-306.**

Nottingham University

Lord Middleton's Lute Book. See: **14.**

Reading

1370 EDWARDS, Warwich. "The Walsingham Consort Books [MSS DDHO/ 20/1-3]," *M&L* 55/2 (1974): 209-14.

IRELAND
Dublin

FITZGIBBON, H. M. "Two Lute Books of Ballet and Dallis," *M&L*   **1371**
XI (1930): 71-77.

WARD, John. "The Lute Books of Trinity College, Dublin: I: MS   **1372**
D.3.30/I. The So-Called Dallis Lute Book," *LSJ* 9 (1967):
17-40.

————. "The Lute Books of Trinity College Dublin: II: MS   **1373**
D.1.2: The So-Called Ballet Lute Book," *LSJ* X (1968): 15-32.

————. "The Fourth Dublin Lute Book," *LSJ* 11 (1969): 28-46.   **1374**

SCOTLAND
Edinburgh

CUTTS, John P. "Seventeenth-Century Songs and Lyrics in Edinburgh   **1375**
University Library Music MS Dc.1.69," *MD* XIII (1959): 169-94.

DAUNEY, W. *Ancient Scottish Melodies from a Manuscript of the*   **1376**
Reign of King James VI. [Adv.5.2.18 (Staloch LB); Adv.5.2.15
(Skene Mandora Book)]. Edinburgh, 1838.

Natl. Lib. Panmure MSS acq. 2763 No. 4. See: **1192: pp. 159-61.**

Natl. Lib. Panmure MSS acq. 2763 No. 5. See: **1192: pp. 115-18.**

Natl. Lib. Panmure MSS acq. 2763 No. 8. See: **1192: pp. 123-26.**

Natl. Lib. Panmure MS 11. See: **14.**

Natl. Lib. Skene MS Adv.5.2.15. See: **506, 1376.**

CZECHOSLOVAKIA

POHANKA, Jarslav. "Loutnove tabulatury z Rajhradského Káštera,"   **1377**
Casopis Moravského Musea XL (1955): 193-203.

Manuscripts

1378   TICHOTA, Jiri. "Tabulatury pro loutnu a pribuzne nástroze na uzemi CSSR," *Acta Universitatis Carolinae Philosophica et Historica* II (1965): 139-49.

Prague

Hudebni Oddeleni Univ. Knihovny ms II Kk 80.   *See:* **1192:** pp. 316-25.

Hudebni Oddeleni Univ. Knihovny ms II Kk 83.   *See:* **1192:** pp. 306-309.

Hudebni Oddeleni Univ. Knihovny ms II Kk 84.   *See:* **1192:** pp. 248-53.

Hudebni Oddeleni Univ. Knihovny ms II Kk 73.   *See:* **1192:** pp. 379-83.

DENMARK
Copenhagen

1379   NEEMAN, Hans. "Laute- und Gitarrehandschrifter in Kopenhagen," *AMl* IV (1932): 129-30.

Gl Kgl. Saml. 377.   *See:* **209, 210, 211.**

Ny Kgl. Saml. 110.   *See:* **209, 210, 211.**

FRANCE
Aix-en-Provence

1380   VERCHALY, André. *Le 'Livre der vers du Luth', manuscrit d'Aix-en-Provence* .... Paris: La Pensee Universitaire, 1958. x + 16p.

Aix-en-Provence Bibl. Mejanes, ms 147 (203) - R312.   *See:* **888, 1192: pp. 163-69.**

Besancon

Bibl. municipal, mss 279.152 (Saizenay ms).   *See:* **1192:** pp. 325-33.

134

Bibl. municipal, ms 279.153 (Saizenay ms). See: **1192: pp. 333-37.**

Paris

ECORECHEVILLE, Jules. "Über die in den Pariser Bibliotheken   **1381**
befindlichen Bestande an Lauten-Tabulaturen," *KONGRESS 1909*, p. 211.

THIBAULT, G. "Un manuscrit italien pour luth des premières   **1382**
années du XVIe siècle [ms T1.1. Biblioteque Thibault] ," in
Le luth et sa musique. Edited by J. Jacquot. Paris: CNRS,
1958, pp. 43-76.

Bibl. Nat., ms Vm7 6211. See: **1192: pp. 133-39.**

Bibl. Nat., ms Vm7 1612 (Monin). See: **1192: pp. 203-12.**

Bibl. Nat., ms Vm7 6213. See: **1192: pp. 212-15.**

Bibl. Nat., ms Vm7 6214. See: **1192: pp. 258-64.**

Bibl. Nat., ms Vm7 6216. See: **1192: pp. 275-77.**

Bibl. Nat., Res 823 (Milleran). See: **1192: pp. 264-70.**

Bibl. Nat., ms Res 1110 (Ruthwen). See: **1192: pp. 197-203.**

Bibl. Nat., Res Vmb ms.7 (Barbe). See: **1192: pp. 277-88.**

Bibl. Nat., Res Vm7 370 (Brossard). See: **1192: pp. 253-58.**

CNRS MS. See: **1192: pp. 109-14.**

*Bibl. Mazarin M.505 (Ballard, P. Tablature du luth, 1631).
See:* **1192: pp. 101-103.**

Bibl. Mazarin: Ballard, P. Tablature . . . . 1638. See: **1192: pp. 103-106.**

Ripon Cathedral MS XVII.B.69. See: **14.**

Manuscripts

Vesoul

1383 BRENET, Michel. "Notice sur deux manuscrits de musique de luth de la Bibliotheque de Vesoul," *Revue d'histoire et de critique musicales* 11/11-12 (1901-1902).

GERMANY
Augsburg

1384 KÜFFNER, Herbert. "Eine Augsburger Sammelhandschrift als Quelle zur Geschichte der Bayreuther Hofmusik," *Archiv für Geschichte von Oberfranken* XLIX (1969): 103-96.

1385 MARTINEZ-GÖLLNER, Marie L. Die Augsburger Bibliothek Herwart und ihre Lautentabulaturen. Ein Musikbestand der Bayerischen Staatsbibliothek aus dem 16. Jahrhundert," *Fontes Artes Musicae* (January-June, 1969), pp. 29-48.

Berlin

1386 NEEMANN, Hans. "Die Lautenhandschrifter von S. L. Weiss in der Bibliothek Dr. W. Wolfheim," *ZfMw* X (1927-1928): 396-414.

1387 SIMON, Alicja. "Die Lautenbestande der Königlich Bibliothek in Berlin," *KONGRESS 1909*, pp. 212-19.

Berlin Deutsche Staatsbibl. Mus. ms 40264. See: **1192:** **pp. 139-44.**

Berlin, Staatliche Museum, Hamilton Collection No. 142 (La Rhetorique des Dieux). See: **1192: pp. 175-79.**

Berlin, Staatsbibl. Preussisscher Kulturbesitz, Musikabt. ms 40068. See: **1192: pp. 193-97.**

Berlin, Staatsbibl. Preussissche Kulturbesitz, Musikabt. ms 40600. See: **1192: pp. 183-88.**

Berlin, Staatsbibl. Preussisscher Kulturbesitz, Musikabt. ms 40601. See: **1192: pp. 362-68.**

Breslau University

SCHNEIDER, Max. "Ein Unbekannte Lautentabulature von 1537-   **1388**
1544," *Festschrift WOLF*, pp. 176-78.

Darmstadt

NOAK, F. "Die Tabulaturen des Hessischen Landesbibliothek zu   **1389**
Darmstadt," *KONGRESS 1924*, pp. 276-85.

Landes und Hochschul Bibliothek, Mus . ms 1655 (no. 3325).
See: 1192: pp. 188-92.

Klosterneuberg

KOCZIRZ, Adolf. "Klosterneuberger Lautenbücher," *Musica*   **1390**
Divina I (1913): 176-77.

Leipzig

Musikbibl. der Staat, ms II 614. See: 1192: pp. 309-16.

Musikbibl. der Staat, ms II 624. See: 1192: pp. 368-79.

Rostock

Univ.-Bibl. Mus. Saec. ms XVIII 18, 54. See: 1192:
pp. 215-27.

Schwerin

Mecklenburgische Landesbibl., Mus. ms 641. See: 1192:
pp. 169-75.

Sorau

TISCHER, G. and K. BURCHARD. "Aus einer alten Bibliothek,"   **1391**
SIMG II (1900-1901): 158-60.

Manuscripts

Zwickau

Ratschulbibl., CXV, 3. See: **1457.**

Prussia

1392 MEIS, Otto. "Elizabethan Music Prints in an East-Prussian Castle," *MD* III (1949): 171-72.

HOLLAND
The Hague

Gemeente Museum-Siena Lute MS. See: **69.**

Gemeente Museum MS 20.860. See: **69.**

HUNGARY
Academy of Sciences

1393 BENKÖ, Daniel. "A Hungarian Lute-Manuscript [K53/II "Istvánffy MS"]," *JLSA* V (1972): 104-109.

ITALY
Genoa

1394 NERI, Achille. "Un codice musicale del secolo XVI [Ms F.VII.1]," *Giornale Storico della Letteratura Italiana* (1886), pp. 218-22.

Lucca

1395 MacCLINTOCK, Carol. "Notes on Four Sixteenth-Century Tuscan Lute Books," *JLSA* IV (1971): 1-8.

1396 ———. "Lucca MS 774—A 16th.-Century Lutebook," paper read in Lawrence Kansas, Mid-West Chapter Meeting, May 1, 1960.

1397 SFORZA, Giovanni. "Poesie musicali del secolo XVI [Lucca MS 774]," *Giornale Storico della Letteratura Italiana* (1886), pp. 312-18.

138

Pesaro

SAVIOTTI, Alfredo. "Di un codice musicale del secolo XVI [Pesaro   1398
MS 1144]," *Giornale Storico della Letteratura Italiana* XIV
(1889):234-52.

PAOLONE, Ernesto. "Codice musicali della Bibl. Oliveriana e della   1399
Bibl. del R. Conservatorio di Musica de Pesaro," *RMI* (1942),
pp. 186-200.

POLAND
Lublin

WINIARSKI, Stanislaw. "Rękopis Nr. 1985 Biblioteki im H.   1400
Łopacińskiego w Lubline," *Muzyka* XVI/3 (1971):87-90.

SPAIN
Madrid

VINDEL, Francesco. *Solaces bibliográficos Madrid.* Madrid: 1401
Instituto Nacional del Libro, 1942, pp. 83-110. [="Libros
españoles sobre la vihuela y ghitarre de los siglos XVI at
XVIII."]

SWEDEN
Kalmar

LINDREN, A. "En tabulaturbok i Kalmar," *Ny Illustrerad Tidning*   1402
for Konst, Bildning och Noje 29/47 (1893):400; 29/48 (1893):
411, 417; 29/50 (1893):436.

Lund

Univ. bibl. Wesnster Litt G 37. See: **1256.**

Norrköping

Stadsbibl. ms "L. de Geer." See: **1192: pp. 144-45.**

Manuscripts

Stockholm

Mus. Akad. MS 32. See: **1439.**

Uppsala

1403 HAMBRAEUS, Bengt. *Codex Carminum Gallicorum; une étude sur le volume "musique vocale du Manuscrit 87" de la Bibliothek de L'Université d'Uppsala.* Uppsala: Almquist and Wiksells, 1961. 158p.

SWITZERLAND
Basel

1404 NEF, Karl. "Die Musik in Basel," Beilage of the *MfM* XXIII (1892): 1-97.

Univ. Bibl. ms F IX 53. See: **1192: pp. 129-32.**

Zurich

Zürcher Zentralbibl. Ms S/26/+2. See: **400.**

U. S. A.
California, Los Angeles

1405 RUBSAMEN, H. "The Taitt Book of Lute Songs," *Festschrift BESSELER*, pp. 259-84.

Oakland

Mills College Cittern Book. See: **14.**

San Francisco

1406 REESE, Gustave. "An Early Seventeenth-Century Italian Lute Manuscript at San Francisco [Bentivoglio Lute MS]," *Festschrift PLAMENAC*, pp. 253-80. *See also:* **1456.**

Connecticut

BOITO, Diane. "Manuscript Music in the . . . Osborn Collection," **1407**
   NOTES 27/2 (December, 1970): 237-44.

STEVENS, Daphne. *The Wickhambrook Lute Manuscript.* Ph.D. **1408**
   diss., published as Collegium Musicum No. 4. New Haven:
   Yale University Department of Music, 1963.

New York, New York Public Library

CUTTS, J. "Songs unto the Violl and Lute [Drexel Ms 4175]," **1409**
   MD XVI (1962): 73-92.

DUCKLES, Vincent. "MS Drexel 4257," *MGG* 4:1348-51. **1410**

———. "The Gamble Manuscript as a Source of Continuo Song **1411**
   in England," *JAMS* I (1948): 23-40.

———. *John Gamble's Commonplace Book.* Unpublished Ph.D. **1412**
   diss., University of California, Berkeley, 1953.

HOLLAND, J. B. "An Eighteenth-Century Lute Manuscript in the **1413**
   New York Public Library," *Bulletin of the New York Public
   Library* 68 (1965): 415-32.

New York, Pierpont Morgan Library

———. "Notes on a Lute Manuscript in the Pierpont Morgan **1414**
   Library," *AMl* (1962), pp. 191-94, (1964), pp. 1-18.

RADKE, Hans. "Wodurch unterscheiden sich Laute und Theorbe," **1415**
   AMl (1965), pp. 73-74.

MUSICAL FORMS

AIR (Ayre, Airs de Cour, *etc.*)

1416 CHILESOTTI, Oscar. "Gli airs de cour di Besard," *KONGRESS 1903*, pp. 131-34.

1417 DODGE, Janet. "Les airs de Cour d'Adrian LeRoy," *Mecure Musicale et Bulletin Français de la SIM* III (November, 1907): 1132-43.

1418 MORROW, Michael. "Ayre on the F♯ String," *LSJ* II (1960): 9-12.

1419 VERCHALY, André. "Les airs italiens mis en tablature de luth dans les recueils français du 17ème siècle," *RM* (July, 1953), pp. 45-77.

1420 ————. "Poésie et air de cour en France jusqu'a 1620," in *Musique et poésie au XVIe siècle.* Edited by J. Jacquot. Paris: CNRS, 1954, pp. 211-24.

1421 WALKER, D. P. "The Influence of 'Musique Mesurée à L'Antique' Particularly on the Airs de Cour of the Early Seventeenth Century," *MD* II (1948): 141-63.

1422 ZUTH, Josef. "Kaiser Josephs I Aria für die Laute," *ZfdG* V (1926): 105ff.

See also: **262, 1431,** Alderman, Pauline. *Antoine Boesset and the Air de Cour.* Unpublished Ph.D. diss., University of Southern California, 1946. 248p.

BASSE-DANSE

1423 SACHS, Curt. "Der Rhythmus der Basse-Danse," *AMl* III (1931): 107-11.

See also: **1433.**

BASSO OSTINATO

1424 GOMBOSI, Otto. "Italia, patria del Basso Ostinato," *RM* VII (1934): 14-25.

1425 PROPPER, L. *Der Basso Ostinato als technisches und formbildendes Prinzip.* Berlin, 1926.

BRANLE

BOGGS, Betty. *The French Branle; Its Origin and Development*   **1426**
before 1700. Unpublished Master's thesis, Indiana University,
1966. 78p.

CANARIO

NELSON, Martha. "Canarios," *GR* 25 (1961): 18-22.   **1427**

CHACONNE

MACHABEY, Armand. "Le origines de la chaconne et de la   **1428**
passacaille," *RMI* (1946), pp. 1-21.

WALKER, Thomas. "Ciaccona and Passacaglia: Remarks on their   **1429**
Origin and Early History," *JAMS* XXI (1968): 300-320.

See also: 933, 1460.

DANCE

CHILESOTTI, Oscar. "La roca el fuso," *RMI* XIX (1912): 361-79.   **1430**

DART, Thurston. "Role de la danse dans l'ayre Anglaise," in   **1431**
Musique et poésie au XVIe siècle. Edited by J. Jacquot. Paris:
CNRS, 1954, pp. 203-10.

GOMBOSI, Otto. "A la recherche de la forme dans la musique de   **1432**
la Renaissance: Francesco da Milano," in *La musique
instrumentale de la Renaissance.* Edited by J. Jacquot. Paris:
CNRS, 1955, pp. 165-76.

HEARTZ, Daniel. "Hoftanz and Basse Danse," *JAMS* XIX   **1433**
(1966): 13-36.

————. *Sources and Forms of the French Instrumental Dance in*   **1434**
the XVIth Century. Unpublished Ph.D. diss., Harvard
University, 1957, pp. 163-41.

1435 HUDSON, Richard. "Chordal Aspects of the Italian Dance Style 1500-1650," *AMl* 42/3-4 (1970): 163-82.

1436 LAUFER, R. *Der Polnische Tanz und sein Endringen in die Kunstmusik*. Unpublished Ph.D. diss., Wien, 1935.

1437 MARKOWSKA, Elzbieta. "Faktura taneczny muzyki lutniowy," *Muzyka* XV (1970): 31-46.

1438 MOE, Lawrence H. *Dance Music in Printed Italian Lute Tablatures from 1507-1611*. Unpublished Ph.D. diss., Harvard University, 1956. 3 vols.

1439 NORLIND, Tobias. "Zur Geschichte der polnischen Tänze," *SIMG* 12 (1910-1911): 501-25.

1440 OPIENSKI, Henryk. "Dawne tance polskie," *Kwartalnik Muzyczny* I (1911): 10ff.

1441 PULVER, Jeffery. "The Ancient Dance Forms," *PRMA* 40 (1914): 73-94.

1442 SCHRADE, Leo. "Tänze aus einer anonymen italienischer tabulatur von 1551," *ZfMw* X (1927-1928): 448-56.

1443 STĘSZEWSKA, Zofia. "Muzyka taneczna taka źródlo Badań miedzynarodowych kontaktów kulturalnych na przykładze polski i francji," *Muzyka* (1972), pp. 39-55.

1444 WARD, John. "The Doleful Domps," *JAMS* IV (1951): 111-21.

See also: Gombosi, Otto. "Der Hoftanz," *AML* VII (1935): 50-61.

FANTASIA

1445 COHEN, Albert. "The Fantaisie for Instrumental Ensemble in 17th-Century France—Its Origin and Significance," *MQ* (1962), pp. 234-43.

1446 KOCZIRZ, Adolf. "Die Fantasien des Melchior de Barberis für die Siebensaitige Gitarre," *ZfMw* IV (1921-1922): 11-17.

MURPHY, R. M. *Fantasia and Ricercar in the 16th Century*. **1447**
Unpublished Ph.D. diss., Yale University, 1954.

————. "Fantasie et Ricercare dans les premières tablatures de luth **1448**
de XVIe siècle," in *Le luth et sa musique*. Edited by J. Jacquot.
Paris: CNRS, 1958, pp. 127-42.

POZNIAK, Z. P. "Wersja kameralna i lutniowa jedny z fantazji **1449**
Diomedesa Catona," *Muzyka* (1969), pp. 79-82.

See also: 51, 160, 198, 519, 1466.

FOLIA

HUDSON, Richard A. "The Folia Dance and the Folia Formula in **1450**
17th-Century Guitar Music," *MD* XXV (1971): 199-222.

FROTTOLA

PIPER, Carla C. *Performance Practice of Italian Frottole*. Unpublished **1451**
Master's project, Stanford University, 1972. 105p.

PRIZER, William F. "Performance Practices in the Frottola," *EM* **1452**
3/3 (1975): 227-35.

GALLIARD

FLOTZINGER, Rudolf. "Die Gagliarda Italiana," *AMl* 39 (1967): **1453**
92-100.

MARKOWSKA, Elzbieta. "Forma Galiarda," *Muzyka* XVI/4 (1971): **1454**
73-85.

————. *Galiardy Thesaurus Harmonicus Besarda jako. žrodło do* **1455**
poznania stylu tanecznej muzyki lutniowej na prziłomie XVI i
XVII wieku. [The Galiard as a Source for Stylistic Information
on Lute Dances of Late 16th- and Early 17th-Century].
Unpublished Ph.D. diss., Warsaw, 1968. 96p.

PETSCHAUER, Roy. *Gagliards of the Bentivoglio Manuscript*. **1456**
Unpublished Master's thesis, San Francisco State College, 1969.
102p.

145

1457 SCHRADE, Leo. "Eine Gagliarde von Cyprian de Rore?" *AfMw* VIII (1926): 385-89.

1458 WENTZEL, Wayne C. *The Lute Galliards of Dowland, Cutting, Holborne and Batchelor.* Unpublished Master's thesis, Harvard University, 1968.

MENUET

1459 TAPPERT, W. "Die Minuita—kein Menuett!," *MfM* 33 (1901): 93-95.

PASSACAGLIA

1460 HUDSON, Richard. "Further Remarks on the Passacaglio and Ciaccona," *JAMS* 23 (1970): 302-14.

1461 ———. "The Ripresa, the Ritornello, and the Passacaglio," *JAMS* 24 (1971): 364-94.

See also: 933, 1428, 1429.

PAVAN

1462 POULTON, Diana. "Notes on the Spanish Pavan," *LSJ* III (1961): 5-16.

PAYSANNE

1463 KLIMA, Josef. "Die paysanne in den österreichischen Lautentabulaturen," *Jahrbuch des Österreichischen Volksliedwerkes* X (1961).

PRELUDE

1464 CURTIS, Alan S. *Unmeasured Preludes in French Baroque Instrumental Music.* Unpublished Master's thesis, University of Illinois, 1956. 147p.

See also: 331.

RICERCAR

OPIENSKI, Henryk. "Quelques considerations sur l'origine des ricercare pour luth," *Festschrift LAURENCIE*, pp. 39-45. **1465**

SLIM, H. Colin. *The Keyboard Ricercar and Fantasia in Italy.* Unpublished Ph.D. diss., Harvard University, 1960. **1466**

See also: 1477, 1448; G. M. da Crema; Toombs.

ROMANCES

BAL Y GAL, Jesús. *Romances y Villancicos españoles del Siglo XVI.* Mexico, 1939. **1467**

KOCZIRZ, Adolf. "Studien zur alten Lautenmusik, altspanischen Romanzen," *Die Gitarre* III (1922): 73ff. **1468**

SACRED MUSIC

DIMSDALE, Verna L. "English Sacred Music with Broken Consort," *LSJ* XIV (1974): 39-64. **1469**

SPRAGUE-SMITH, C. "Religious Music and the Lute," *GR* 9 (1949): 31-37. **1470**

See also: 106.

SARABAND

DEVOTO, Daniel. "La folle sarabande," *RMl* XLV (1960): 3-43, 145-80. **1471**

————. "De la zarabanda a la sarabande," *Recherches sur la musique française classique* VI (1966): 27-72. **1472**

ESCUDERO, José C. "Quelques additions a 'La folle sarabande'," *RMl* (1961), pp. 117-25. **1473**

HUDSON, Richard A. "The Zarabanda and Zarabanda Francese in Italian Guitar Music of the Early 17th Century," *MD* 24 (1970): 125-50. **1474**

Musical Forms

1475 PRUSIK, K. "Die Sarabande in der Solopartien des Lautenisten S. L. Weiss," *Festschrift KOCZIRZ*, pp. 36-37.

1476 STEVENSON, R. "A Propos de la sarabande," *RMI* (1961): 113-17.

SONG

1477 BOETTICHER, Wolfgang. "On Vulgar Music and Poetry Found in Unexplored Minor Sources of Eighteenth-Century Lute Tablatures," *Festschrift GEIRINGER*, pp. 76-85.

1478 BONTOUX, G. *La chanson en angleterre au temps d'Elizabeth.* Oxford: Oxford University Press, 1936. 699p.

1479 CHILESOTTI, Oscar. "Canzonette del seicento con la chitarra," *RMI* XVI (1909): 847-62.

1480 ———. "Chansons françaises du XVIe siècle en italie (transcrites pour luth)," *Revue d'histoire et de critique musicales* II (1902): 63, 202ff.

1481 CYR, Mary. "Song Accompaniment for the Lyra Viol and Lute," *JLSA* IV (1971): 43-49.

1482 EMSLIE, McD. "Nicholas Lanier's Innovations in English Song," *M&L* 41 (1960): 13-27.

1483 FORTUNE, Nigel. "Polyphonic Italian Madrigals of the Seventeenth Century," *M&L* XLVII (1966): 153-59.

1484 ———. "Solo Song [with Lute Accompaniment in Europe]," *NOHM* vol. 4, pp. 126-30, 184-89, 191-94, 200-17.

1485 FOX, Charles W. "Ein Fröhlich Wesen: The Career of a German Song in the Sixteenth Century," *Papers Read at the AMS*, 1937, pp. 56-74.

1486 GÉROLD, Théodore. *L'art du chant en france au XVIIe siècle.* Strasbourg: Commission des Publications de la Faculté des Lettres, Palais de L'Université, 1921, pp. 110-31.

1487 GREER, David. "The Lute Songs of Thomas Morley," *LSJ* VIII (1966): 25-37.

————. "The Part-Songs of the English Lutenists," *PRMA* (1967-1968), pp. 97-110.   **1488**

JUDD, Percy. "The Songs of John Danyel," *M&L* XVII (1936): 118-23.   **1489**

KINGSLEY, Victoria. "The Words Do Matter," *LSJ* XII (1970): 37ff.   **1490**

KLIMA, Josef. "Das Volkslied vor 1800 und die Lautentabulaturen," *Jahrbuch der Österreichischen Volksliedwerks* XVI (1967): 61-66.   **1491**

LAMSON, Roy. "English Broadside Ballad Tunes of the 16th- and 17th Centuries," *KONGRESS 1939*, pp. 112-21.   **1492**

LAND, J. P. N. "De Luit en het Wereldlijke Lied in Duitschland en Nederland," *Tijdschrift voor Noord Nederlansche Muziekgeschiedenis* IV (1894): 17-32.   **1493**

PALISCA, Claude. "Vincenzo Galilei and Some Links Between 'Pseudo-Monody' and 'Monody'," *MQ* XLVI (1960): 344-60.   **1494**

PATTERSON, A. W. "The XVIth-Century Lute Songs," *MT* 86 (1930): 796-98.   **1495**

POULTON, Diana. "John Dowland's Songs and Their Instrumental Settings," *MMR* 81 (1951): 175-80.   **1496**

RADECKE, Ernst. "Das deutsche weltliche Lied in der Lautenmusik des 16. Jahrhunderts," *VfMw* VII (1891): 286-336.   **1497**

RAYNOR, Henry. "Framed to the Life of the Words," *Music Review* 19 (1958): 261-72.   **1498**

SCHNEIDER, Max. "Zur Geschichte des Begleiteten Sologesangs," *Festschrift KRETZSCHMAR*, pp. 138-49.   **1499**

SPINK, Ian. "English Cavalier Songs, 1620-1660," *PRMA* 86 (1960): 61-78.   **1500**

————. *English Song: Dowland to Purcell.* New York: Charles Scribner's Sons, 1974. 312p.   **1501**

Musical Forms

1502 STEVENS, Denis. "German Lute Songs of the Early Sixteenth Century," *Festschrift BESSELER*, pp. 253-57.

1503 TEGNELL, John C. *Elizabethan Prosody: A Study of the Style of the English Madrigal and Ayre.* Unpublished Ph.D. diss., Northwestern University, 1949. 248p.

1504 WARD, John. "Music for a Handfull of Pleasant Delites," *JAMS* X (1957):151-80.

1505 WELLS, Robin H. "The Art of Persuasion (Come Again/Dowland)," *LSJ* XIV (1974):67-69.

SPAGNOLETTA

1506 PETSCHAUER, Roy. "Three Spagnolettas from the Bentivoglio Manuscript," *GR* 32 (1969):5-11.

SUITE

1507 BLUME, F. *Studien zur Vorgeschichte der Orchestersuite im 15. und 16. Jahrhunderts.* Leipzig, 1925.

1508 NORLIND, Tobias. "Zur Geschichte der Suite," *SIMG* VII (1905-1906): 172-203.

1509 REIMANN, Hugo. "Zur Geschichte der deutschen Suite," *SIMG* VI (1904):504-10, 512, 515-20.

See also: 514.

TOCCATA

1510 GOMBOSI, Otto. "Zur Vorgeschichte der Toccate," *AMl* VI (1934): 49-53.

1511 SCHRADE, Leo "Ein Beiträge zur Geschichte der Tokkate," *ZfMw* VIII (1925):610-35.

TOMBEAU

BRENET, Michel. "Les tombeaux en musique," *Revue musicale*   **1512**
pp. 568-75, 631-38.

DUCKLES, Vincent. "The English Musical Elegy of the Late   **1513**
Renaissance," in *Aspects of Medieval and Renaissance Music.*
Edited by Jan LaRue. New York: Norton, 1966, pp. 134-53.

ROLLIN, Monique. "Le 'Tombeau' chez les luthistes D. Gaultier,   **1514**
J. Gallot, Charles Mouton," *Revue de la société d'étude au
XVIIe siècle* 21-22 (1954): 436ff.

VARIATIONS

HORSLEY, Imogene. *Instrumental Variations Before 1580.*   **1515**
Unpublished Ph.D. diss., Radcliffe, 1954.

————. "The Sixteenth-Century Variation and Baroque   **1516**
Counterpoint," *MD* XIV (1960): 161-68.

————. "The 16th-Century Variation: A New Historical Survey,"   **1517**
JAMS XII (1959): 118-32.

HUGHES, J. *The Tientos, Fugas and Diferencias in Antonio de   **1518**
Cabezon's Obras de Musica Para Tecla, Harpa y Vihuela.*
Unpublished Ph.D. diss., Florida State University, 1961.

VILLANCICO

SCHNEIDER, Marius. "Un villancico de Alonso de Mudarra   **1519**
procedente a de la musica popular granadina," *AnM* 10 (1955):
79-83.

See also: **1467**.

VILLANELLA

CHILESOTTI, Oscar. "Villanella a 3 voci del 'Thesaurus   **1520**
Harmonicus' di G. B. Besardo (1603)," *Festschrift REIMANN*,
pp. 287-88.

RELATED INSTRUMENTS

ALMERIQUE

1521 KNOWLSON, J. R. "Jean le Maire, the Almerie and the Musique Almerique: a Set of Unpublished Documents," *AMI* 40 (1968): 86-90.

ANGELIQUE

1522 LESURE, François. "The Angelique in 1653," *GSJ* VI (1953): 111-12.

See also: 914.

BANDORA

1523 GILL, Donald. "Descriptions of the Bandora, Penorcon and Orpharion from Praetorius, William Barley, Trichet MS and Talbot MS," *LSJ* II (1960): 39ff.

1524 ———. "The Sources of English Solo Bandora Music," *LSJ* IV (1962): 23-27.

See also: 1541.

CHITARRA BATTANTE

1525 SACHS, Curt. "Die Streichbogenfrage," *AfMw* I (1919): 1-9.

COBZA [Kobza]

1526 LAVROV, F. "Ukrainski Kobzor' Ostap Veresoi," *Sovietskaja Muzyka* IV (1954): 86-91.

1527 LLOYD, A. L. "The Rumanian Cobza," *LSJ* II (1960): 13-16.

COLASCIONE

1528 FRYKLUND, O. "Colascione och Colascionister," *Slöjd och Ton* 18 (1936): 88ff.

152

LÜCK, R. *Ein Beiträge zur Geschichte des Colascione und seiner*   **1529**
süddeutschen Tondenksmäler im 18. Jahrhundert. Unpublished
Ph.D. diss., Erlangen, 1954.

————. "Zur Geschichte der Basslauten-Instrumente Colascione   **1530**
und Calichon," *Deutsches Jahrbuch der Musikwissenschaft*
für 1960. Edited by W. Vetter. Leipzig, 1961, pp. 67-75.

————. "Zwei unbekannte Basslauten-Instrumente, der italienische   **1531**
Colascione und der deutsche Galichon," *Neue Zeitschrift für*
Musik CXXVI (1965): 10-13.

See also: 917.

MANDOLA

See: 917.

MANDOLIN

RANIERI, M. S. "Mandoline," in *Encyclopédie de la Musique*.   **1532**
Edited by Lavignac. Paris, 1931, pp. 1991-96.

REINHARD, Kurt. "Mandoline," *MGG* 8:1572-74.   **1533**

SAINT-FOIS, G. de. "Un fonds inconnu de composition pour   **1534**
mandoline (XVIIIe siècle)," *RMI* 14 (1933): 129-35.

VAN TEESELING, D. "Das Mandolinenspiel in den Niederlanden,"   **1535**
Die Volksmusik edition B (1939): 261ff.

WÖLKI, Konrad. *Die Geschichte der Mandoline*. Berlin, 1940.   **1536**

ZUTH, Josef. "Johann Adolf Hasses Concerto con Mandolino,"   **1537**
Muse des Saitenspiels XIII (1931): 72ff.

See also: 898.

MANDORA

KOCZIRZ, Adolf. "Albrechtsbergers Konzerte für Maultrommel und   **1538**
Mandora," *Festschrift KRETZSCHMAR*, pp. 55-57.

Reviews

1539 REINHARD, Kurt. "Mandol-Mandora," *MGG* 8:1571-72.

See also: 287, 939, 1117: pp. 482-89.

MANDORLAUTE

1540 KOCZIRZ, Adolf. "Zur Geschichte der Mandorlaute," *Die Gitarre* II (1920): 21ff.

ORPHARION

1541 GILL, Donald. "The Orpharion and Bandora," *GSJ* 13 (1960): 14-25.

1542 ――――. "An Orpharion by John Rose," *LSJ* II (1960): 33-40.

1543 HADAWAY, Robert. "An Instrument-Maker's Report on the Repair and Restoration of an Orpharion," *GSJ* 28 (1975): 32-42.

See also: 1075, 1523, 1650.

PANDORA

See: 1075, 1076.

PENORCON

See: 1523.

QUINTERNE

See: 917.

REVIEWS

1544 *Airs de Cour* . . . . Verchaly, A.
REV: Heartz, D. *JAMS* 15 (1962).

1545 ALBERT de RIPPE. *Oeuvres, Bk. I.*
REV: Dobbins, F. *M&L* 55 (1974): 247.

ALBERT de RIPPE. *Oeuvres, Bk. I.*   **1546**
REV: Kanazawa, M. *NOTES* 32 (1975): 131-32.

Das Allgäu . . . . Layer, A.   **1547**
REV: Kolneder, R. *Mf* 23/1 (1970): 109.

ATTAIGNANT, P. *Preludes, Chansons* . . . . Heartz, D. (ed.).   **1548**
REV: O., G. S. *GSJ* 20 (1967): 103-105.

ATTAIGNANT, P. *Preludes* . . . . Heartz, D. (ed.).   **1549**
REV: Radke, H. *Mf* 20/1 (1964): 112-14.

ATTAIGNANT, P. *Preludes* . . . . Heartz, D. (ed.).   **1550**
REV: Sutton, J. *NOTES* 25/3 (1969): 574-82.

BACHELER, D. *Selected Wks.* Long, M. (ed.).   **1551**
REV: Beechey, G. *M&L* 54/4 (1973): 508-11.

BACHELER, D. *Selected Wks.* Long (ed.).   **1552**
REV: Kanazawa, M. *NOTES* 32/1 (1975): 131-32.

BALLARD, R. *Oeuvres* . . . (*1611*). Souris (ed.).   **1553**
REV: O., G. S. *GSJ* 20 (1967): 103ff.

Beiträge zur Geschichte . . . *Lautenmacher.* Malacek, A.   **1554**
REV: Anon. *Mf* 11 (1958): 99.

BESARD, J. B. *Oeuvres* . . . . Souris (ed.).   **1555**
REV: Anon. *IFr* no. 5 (1973): 29-31.

BOTTEGARI, E. *Lute Book.* MacClintock (ed.).   **1556**
REV: Porter, W. *JAMS* 20/1 (1967): 126-31.

BOTTEGARI, E. *Lute Book.* MacClintock (ed.).   **1557**
REV: Radke, H. *Mf* 21/1 (1968): 135-36.

BOTTEGARI, E. *Lute Book.* MacClintock (ed.).   **1558**
REV: Sutton, J. *NOTES* 25/3 (1969): 579-82.

Burwell Lute Book. Spencer, R. (ed.).   **1559**
REV: Buetens, S. *JLSA* 7 (1974): 104-107.

Reviews

1560 *Burwell Lute Book.* Spencer, R. (ed.)
REV: Simpson, A. *EM* 3/2 (1975): 165.

1561 CHANCY. *Oeuvres.* Souris (ed.).
REV: Brown, H. *NOTES* 25/3 (1969): 576-77.

1562 CHANCY. *Oeuvres.* Souris (ed.).
REV: Verchaly, A. *RMl* 54 (1968): 135-36.

1563 *Codex Carminum* .... Hambraeus, B.
REV: Anon. *MT* 103 (1962): 475ff.

See also: Musica 16 (1962): 165.

1564 CURTIS, J. (Dir.). *Renaissance of the Cittern-MHS 1891.*
REV: Buetens, S. *JLSA* 7 (1974): 109-10.

1565 DANNER, Peter. "Some Observations on Recent Editions of Lute Music,"
LSJ II (1969): 48-54.

1566 DOMBOIS, E. *Music for Baroque Lute, Ph 657-5005.*
REV: Scott, D. *MT* (May, 1975), pp. 447.

1567 DOWLAND, J. *Collected Lute Music.* Poulton (ed.).
REV: Danner, P. *JLSA* 8 (1975): 95-98.

1568 DOWLAND, J. *Lachrimae.* Facs. ed.
REV: Anon. *M&L* 56/2 (1975).

1569 DOWLAND, J. *Lachrimae.* Facs. ed.
REV: Harwood, I. *EM* 3/2 (1975): 159, 161.

1570 DUFAUT. *Oeuvres.* Souris (ed.).
REV: O., G. S. *GSJ* 20 (1967): 103ff.

1571 DUFAUT. *Oeuvres.* Souris (ed.).
REV: Radke, H. *Mf* 21 (1968): 136-38.

1572 *English Lute Songs, 1597-1632* .... Sternfeld (gen. ed.).
REV: S., G. *LSJ* 11 (1969): 52-54.

1573 *English Madrigal Verse* .... 3rd. ed., Fellowes, E., Sternfeld (ed.).
REV: S., G. *LSJ* 11 (1969): 55-56.

English Song .... Spink, I.   **1574**
   REV: Duckles, V. *JAMS* 28/3 (1975): 549-52.

English Song Dowland to Purcell. Spink, I.   **1575**
   REV: Anon. *LSJ* 14 (1974): 72-74.

English Song-Books, 1651 .... Day, C. and E. Boswell.   **1576**
   REV: Anon. *M&L* 22 (1941): 288ff.

Das Florilegium ... *Denss.* Klöckner, D.   **1577**
   REV: Anon. *Mf* 24/2 (1971): 195-96.

Das Florilegium ... *Denss.* Klöckner, D.   **1578**
   REV: Lobaugh, H. B. *JLSA* 5 (1972): 110-14.

Francesco da Milano: Opere Complete .... Chiesa (ed.).   **1579**
   REV: Danner, P. *JLSA* 5 (1972): 117-21.

FRANCESCO da MILANO. *Lute Music of* .... Ness (ed.).   **1580**
   REV: Danner, P. *JLSA* 4 (1971): 56-59.

GAULTIER, E. *Oeuvres* .... Souris (ed.).   **1581**
   REV: Anon. *Mf* 22/1 (1969): 141-43.

GAULTIER, E. *Oeuvres* .... Souris (ed.).   **1582**
   REV: Verchaly, A. *RMl* 53/1 (1967): 88.

Geigen-und Lautenmacher .... Lütgendorff, W.   **1583**
   REV: D., F. d. "Viol och lutmakare ... ," *STfM* (1922): 101-108.

GOSTENA, G. B. *Intavolatura* .... Gullino (ed.).   **1584**
   REV: Anon. *GSJ* (1950), p. 55.

Guitar from the Renaissance .... Turnbull, H.   **1585**
   REV: Cox, P. *NOTES* 31/4 (1975): 786-87.

Guitar from the Renaissance .... Turnbull, H.   **1586**
   REV: Danner, P. *MT* (August, 1975), p. 709.

Handbuch der Laute und Gitarre. Zuth, J.   **1587**
   REV: Lach, R. *ZfMw* 11 (1928-1929): 185ff.

1588 HOLBORNE, A. *Complete Wks., Bk. I.* Kanazawa (ed.).
REV: Anon. *NOTES* 25/3 (1969): 577-79.

1589 HOLBORNE, A. *Complete Wks., Bk. I.* Kanazawa (ed.).
REV: Jeffrey, B. *JAMS* 22 (1969): 125-26.

1590 HOLBORNE, A. *Complete Wks., Bk. II.* Kanazawa (ed.).
REV: Harwood, I. *EM* 3/2 (1975): 165, 167, 169.

1591 *John Dowland.* Poulten, D.
REV: Buetens, S. *JLSA* 4 (1971): 59-63.

1592 *John Dowland.* Poulton, D.
REV: Greer, D. *M&L* 55/1 (1974): 99-100.

1593 *John Dowland.* Poulton, D.
REV: R., A. *LSJ* 14 (1972): 55.

1594 JOHNSON, R. *Complete Wks.* Sundermann (ed.).
REV: Beechey, G. *M&L* 54 (1973): 508-11.

1595 JOHNSON, R. *Complete Wks.* Sundermann (ed.).
REV: Kanazawa, M. *NOTES* 32/1 (1975): 131-32.

1596 KOCZIRZ, A. "Neuausgaben alter Lautenmusik," *Die Gitarre* 4/6 (1923).

1597 *Laute, Theorbe* .... Pohlmann, E.
REV: Anon. *JLSA* 5 (1972): 114-16.

1598 *Laute, Theorbe* .... Pohlmann, E.
REV: Rooley, A. *EM* 3/2 (1975): 157.

1599 *Laute und Gitarre.* Sommer, H.
REV: Brondi, M. R. *RMI* 29 (1922): 659ff.

1600 *Die Lautentabulaturen ... Kremsmünster.* Flotzinger, R.
REV: Anon. *Mf* 21/2 (1968): 242-44.

1601 *Die Lautentabulaturen* .... Flotzinger, R.
REV: Anon. *Erasmus* 19 (1967): 551-52.

Die Lautentabulaturen .... Flotzinger, R.   1602
REV: Verchaly, A. *RMI* 53/1 (1967):69-70.

Le luth et sa musique. Jacquot (ed.).   1603
REV: Bloch, S. *NOTES* 17 (1960):403-404.

LeROY, A. *Fantaisies* ... (*1568*). Souris (ed.).   1604
REV: Jansen, P. *M&L* 44 (1963):91-92.

LeROY, A. *Première Livre* ... (*1551*). Souris (ed.).   1605
REV: Anon. *RMI* 48 (1962):182-84.

LeROY, A. *Psaumes:* ... (*1552*). Morcourt (ed.).   1606
REV: Anon. *M&L* 44 (1963):308-309.

Il Liuto .... Brondi, M. R.   1607
REV: La Laurencie, L. de. *RMI* 9 (1927):51ff.

Liuto, Vihuela, chitarra .... Tonazzi, B.   1608
REV: Heck, T. *JLSA* 6 (1973):63-65.

Lute Construction. Cooper, R.   1609
REV: Harwood, I. *GSJ* 19 (1966):157-59.

Lute Making. Bachorik, J.   1610
REV: Elder, L. *JLSA* 8 (1975):98-100.

Lute Music of Shakespeare's Time/Barley's New Booke of Tablature   1611
(*1596*). Newcomb (ed.).
REV: Dart, T. *JAMS* 20/3 (1967):493-95.

Lyrics from English Airs.... Doughtie (ed.).   1612
REV: Greer, D. *M&L* 55/1 (1974):108-109.

Meine Laute. Sörnsen, N.   1613
REV: Brondi, M. R. *RMI* 32 (1925):131ff.

Method for the Renaissance Lute. Buetens, S.   1614
REV: Garton, J. *JLSA* 2 (1969):56.

MILAN, Luis. *El Maestro.* Jacobs (ed.).   1615
REV: Heck, T. *JAMS* 25 (1972):487-90.

Reviews

1616   MILAN, Luis. *Libro de Musica.* Schrade (ed.).
REV: Gombosi, O. *ZfMw* (1931-1932), pp. 185, 189.

1617   MILAN, Luis. Leo Schrade's reply to Gombosi's review. *ZfMw*
19 (1931-1932): 357-63.

1618   MINKIN, D. *John Dowland: Lute Songs . . . . MHS 1548.*
REV: Danner, P. *JLSA* 6 (1973): 68-70.

1619   "Modality in Spanish Vihuela . . . ." *AnM* 26 (1972): 29-59, Grebe, M. E.
REV: Stevenson, R. *Rivista Musical Chilena* 28 (1974): 98-99.

1620   MOLINARO, S. *Intavolatura . . . .* Gullino (ed.).
REV: Roncaglia, G. *RMI* 44 (1940): 184ff.

1621   *Music for the Lute.* Lumsden (gen. ed.). Elizabethan Pop. Music, Bk. I;
Cutting, Bk. 2; Pilkington, Bk. 3; Johnson, Bk. 4; Bachelor, Bk. 5.
OUP, 1968-1972.
REV: Harwood, I. *LSJ* 15 (1973): 54-56.

1622   NEWSIDLER, H. *Ein Newgeordent . . . (1536).* Facs. ed.
REV: Danner, P. *JLSA* 7 (1974): 103-104.

1623   RADINO, G. M. *Intavolatur di balli . . . .* Gullino (ed.).
REV: Anon. *GSJ* (1950), pp. 55-56.

1624   RAGOSSNIG, K. *Musik für Laute,* vol. 1 & 2, Archiv 2533 157/2533 173.
REV: Heck, T. *JLSA* 8 (1975), pp. 100-102.

1625   RHODES, D. *Sonatas of S. L. Weiss.* Cambridge CRS 2301.
REV: Smith, D. A. *JLSA* 6 (1973): 66-67.

1626   ROBINSON, T. *Schoole of Musicke (1603).* Lumsden (ed.).
REV: Buetens, S. *JLSA* 5 (1972): 116-17.

1627   ROBINSON, T. *Schoole of Musicke (1601).* Lumsden (ed.).
REV: S., R. *LSJ* 15 (1973): 51-54.

1628   ROOLEY, A. and TYLER, J. *Renaissance Duets.* L'Oiseau Lyre SOL 325.
REV: S., A. M. *LSJ* 14 (1972): 56.

1629   *Sang und Klang . . . .* Tappert, W. (ed.).
REV: Koczirz, A. *ZIMG* 8 (1907): 228ff.

SANZ, G. "Gaspar Sanz. An Overview of Various Editions." Artzt, A.   **1630**
  GR 40 (1976): 33.

Sampson Lute Book. Spencer (ed.).   **1631**
  REV: Buetens, S. *JLSA* 7 (1974): 104-107.

Sampson Lute Book. Spencer (ed.).   **1632**
  REV: Rooley, A. *EM* 3/2 (1975): 163, 165.

SATOH, T. *Baroque Lute Recital*. Klavier, KS 514, KS 528.   **1633**
  REV: Purcell, R. and Lyons, D. *JLSA* 7 (1974): 107-109.

SATOH, T. *Baroque Lute Recital*. KS 514, KS 528.   **1634**
  REV: S., A. M. *LSJ* 14 (1972): 55-56.

Schule des Lautenspiels. Bruger, H. (ed.).   **1635**
  REV: Brondi, M. R. *RMI* 32 (1925): 471.

Studien zur Lautenmusik . . . . Dorfmuller, K.   **1636**
  REV: Radke, H. *Mf* 28/1 (1970): 65-70.

Turpyn Lute Book. Rastall (ed.).   **1637**
  REV: Anon. *M&L* 56/2 (1975).

Turpyn Lute Book. Rastall (ed.).   **1638**
  REV: Buetens, S. *JLSA* 7 (1974): 104-107.

Turpyn Lute Book. Rastall (ed.).   **1639**
  REV: Scott, D. *LSJ* 15 (1973): 56-60.

Turpyn Lute Book. Rastall (ed.).   **1640**
  REV: Simpson, A. *EM* 3/2 (1975): 161, 163.

VALLET, N. *Oeuvres* . . . (*1615, 1616*). Souris (ed.).   **1641**
  REV: Buetens, S. *JLSA* 3 (1970): 69-72.

WEISS, S. L. *Intavolatura* . . . . Chiesa (ed.).   **1642**
  REV: P., D. *LSJ* 11 (1969): 49-52.

Wickhambrook Lute Book. Stevens, D. (ed.).   **1643**
  REV: Murphy, R. *NOTES* 23/4 (1967): 826.

1644 *Von den Anfängen der Lautenmusik*. Engel, E.
REV: Wolf, J. *ZfMw* 2 (1919-1920): 669.

TABLATURE / TRANSCRIPTION

1645 APEL, W. *The Notation of Polyphonic Music 900-1600*. Cambridge,
Massachusetts: Medieval Academy of America. 4th ed., 1949,
pp. 51-81.

1646 BAL Y GAL, Jesús. "Fuenllana and the Transcription of Spanish Lute
Music," *AMl* 11 (1939): 16-27.

1647 BARON, Ernst G. "Abhandlung von dem Notensystem der Laute und der
Theorbe," in Marburg, *Historische-Kritische Beiträge*, vol. 2. Berlin:
Lange, 1756, pp. 119-23.

1648 BLOCH, S. "Lutemusic, its Notation and Technical Problems in Relation
to the Guitar," *GR* 9 (1949): 15-18.

1649 BOETTICHER, Wolfgang. "Notation," *MGG* 9:1641-48.

1650 BUETENS, Stanley (ed.). *The First Book of Tablature: for Lute, Guitar,
Orpharion*. New York: Instrumenta Antiqua Publications, 1964.

1651 BUGGERT, R.W. "Transcription Problems in the Lute Tablature Books
of Alberto da Ripa," in *Wichita University Studies* Nr 34,
August 31, 1956.

1652 CHILESOTTI, Oscar. "L'evoluzione nella scrittura dei suoni musicali,"
RMI 8 (1901): 130-36.

1653 ———. "Notes sur la tablature de luth et de guitare," in *Encyclopédie
de la musique*. Edited by Lavignac. Paris, 1931, pp. 636-84.

1654 DISERTORI, B. "Contradiction tonale dans la transcription d'un
Strambotto Célèbre," in *Le luth et sa musique*. Edited by J. Jacquot.
Paris: CNRS, 1958, pp. 37-42.

1655 DORFMÜLLER, Kurt. "La tablature de luth allemande et les problèms
d'édition," *Le luth et sa musique*. Edited by J. Jacquot. Paris: CNRS,
1958, pp. 245-58.

GERMESIN, Elfi. *Zum Problem der Intavolierung mehrstimmer*   **1656**
vokalmusik im 16. und frühen 17. Jahrhundert. Ph.D. diss.,
Saarbrücken, forthcoming.

GIESBERT, F. J. "Die deutsche Tabulaturen für Lauten und Geygen,"   **1657**
Der Blockflöten Spiegel 3/4 (1930).

GOMBOSI, Otto. "Bemerkungen zum Problem der Lautentabulatur-   **1658**
Übertragung," *ZfMw* 16 (1933):497-98.

————. "Bemerkungen zur Lautentabulaturfrage," *ZfMw* 15   **1659**
(1932):357.

HAYES, Gerald. "Instruments and Instrumental Notation," in   **1660**
NOHM vol. 4, pp. 721-26, 773-78.

HECK, Thomas. "Lute Music: Tablatures, Textures and   **1661**
Transcriptions," *JLSA* 7 (1974):19-30.

HUELTBERG, W. Earle. "Transcription of Tablature to Standard   **1662**
Notation," in *The Computer and Music.* Edited by Harry B.
Lincoln. Ithaca, New York: Cornell University Press, 1970,
pp. 288-92.

KIESEWETTER, R. G. "Die Tabulaturen der älteren Praktiker seit   **1663**
der Einführung des Figural- und Mensuralgesanges des
Contrapunctes," *Allgemeine Musikalische Zeitung* 33 (1831):
33-38, 134-48.

KOCZIRZ, Adolf. "Lauten- und Orgel-tabulaturen," in *Handbuch*   **1664**
der Musikgeschichte. Edited by G. Adler, 1930, vol. 1:398-408.

————. "Über die Notwendigkeit eines unheitlichen, wissen-   **1665**
schaftlichen und instrumentalnischen Forderungen ensprechenden
Systems in der Übertragung von Lautentabulatur," *KONGRESS*
1909, pp. 220-23.

MEYLAN, Raymond. "La technique de transcription au luth de   **1666**
Francesco Spinacino," *Schweitzer Beiträge zu Musikwissenschaft*
1 (1972):83-93.

1667 MOE, Lawrence H. "Le problème des barres de mesure dans les tablatures de luth du XVIe siècle," in *Le luth et sa musique*. Edited by J. Jacquot. Paris: CNRS, 1958, pp. 259-76.

1668 NELSON, John C. *Johannes Wolf's Handbuch der Notationskunde*. A Translation and Critical Commentary. Unpublished Ph.D. diss., Iowa State University, 1964. *See also:* **1684**.

1669 NOSKE, Frits. "Two Problems in Seventeenth-Century Notation," *AMl* 27 (1955): 113-20.

1670 PATTISON, Bruce. "Notes on Early Music Printing," *The Library* 4th ser. 19/4 (1934): 389-421.

1671 PFENNINGS, Isolde. Importancia de las instrumentos de cuerdas punteadas y sus tablaturas," *Rivista Musical Chilena* (1960), pp. 34-43.

1672 PODOLSKI, Michel. "A la recherche d'une methode de transcription formelle de tablatures de luth," in *Le luth et sa musique*. Edited by J. Jacquot. Paris: CNRS, 1958, pp. 277-84.

1673 POŽNIAK, Piotr. "Z zagadnien transkrypcji muzyki lutniowej," *Muzyka* 12/2 (1967): 3-10.

1674 PRYNNE, Michael W. "Comment noter et conserver les mesures de luths anciens," in *Le luth et sa musique*. Edited by J. Jacquot. Paris: CNRS, 1958, pp. 239-44.

1675 PUJOL, E. "La transcription de la tablature pour vihuela d'après la technique de l'instrument," *KONGRESS 1936*.

1676 RADKE, H. "Beiträge zur Erforchung der Lautentabulaturen des 16. - 18. Jahrhunderts," *Mf* 16 (1963): 34-51.

1677 ———. "Zum Problem der Lautentabulatur-Übertragung," *AMl* 43 (1971): 94-103.

1678 ROTTNER, Les R. *The Intabulation Practises of Vincenzo Capirola with Special Emphasis on Musica Ficta*. Unpublished Master's thesis, University of Hartford, Connecticut, 1967. 75p.

SCHMITZ, E. "Über Gitarretabulaturen," *MfM* 35 (1903):133-47.   **1679**

SCHRADE, Leo. "Das Problem der Lautentabulatur Übertragung,"   **1680**
ZfMz (1931), pp. 357-62.

SOURIS, André. "Tablature et Syntaxe: Remarques sur le rôle des   **1681**
transcriptions de tablatures de luth," in *Le luth et sa musique*.
Edited by J. Jacquot. Paris: CNRS, 1958, pp. 285-96.

TAPPERT, W. "Zur Geschichte der französischen Lautentabulatur,"   **1682**
Allgemeine Deutsche Musikzeitung 13 (1886-1887):140ff.

VERCHALY, André. "La tabulature dans les recueils français   **1683**
pour chant et luth, 1603-1643," in *Le luth et sa musique*.
Edited by J. Jacquot. Paris: CNRS, 1958, pp. 155-69.

WOLF, Johannes. *Handbuch der Notationskunde*, vol. 2 repr.   **1684**
Hamburg: G. Olms Verlag, 1963. *See also:* **1668**.

————. Über Gitarretabulaturen," *KONGRESS 1911*, p. 354.   **1685**

ZUTH, Josef. "Aufsätze: Griff- und Akkord Notation," *Der Merker*   **1686**
9/4 (1918).

See also: **552, 577**.

THEORBO

Anon. "Literatur für die Barocklaute," *Hausmusik* 24 (1960):146.   **1687**

BUETENS, Stanley. "Theorbo Accompaniments of Early Seventeenth-   **1688**
Century Italian Monody," *JLSA* 6 (1973):37-45.

DUNCAN, Edmondstowne. "Of the Lute or Theorbo," *MMR* 32   **1689**
(1902):65.

GODWIN, Jocelyn. "Survival of the Theorbo Principle," *JLSA* 6   **1690**
(1973):4-16.

JONES, Edwary Huws. "The Theorbo and Continuo Practise in the   **1691**
Early English Baroque," *GSJ* 25 (1971):67-72.

1692 NEEMANN, Hans. "Laute und Theorbe als Generalbass-instrument im 17. und 18. Jahrhundert," *ZfMw* 15 (1934): 527-34.

1693 QUITTARD, Henri. "Le theorbe comme instrument d'accompagnement," *Le Mercure Musicale de SIM* (1910), pp. 222-37, 362-84.

1694 RADKE, Hans. "Theorbierte Laute und Erzlaute," *Mf* 25/4 (1972): 481-84.

See also: 1022, 1090, 1139.

TUNING / ORNAMENTS

1695 BARBER, J. Murry. *Tuning and Temperment. A Historical Survey.* Michigan, 1953.

1696 BRUGER, Hans. "Fis stimmung oder 'Normalstimmung' für die Laute?" *Die Musikantengilde* 3/2 (1924).

1697 CHARNASSÉ, Hélène. "Sur l'accord de la guitare," *Recherches sur la musique française classique* 7 (1967): 25-38.

1698 DAVID, Hans. "An Italian Tablature Lesson on the Renaissance," paper read at annual meeting of the AMS, Boston, December 27, 1958.

1699 DOBSON, Charles, Ephraim SEGERMAN and James TYLER. "The Tunings of the Four-Course French Cittern and of the Four-Course Guitar in the 16th Century," *LSJ* 16 (1974): 17-23.

1700 DODGE, J. "Ornamentation as Indicated by Signs in Lute Tablature," *SIMG* 9 (1907-1908): 318-36.

1701 DOMBOIS, Eugen M. "Varieties of Meantone Temperment Realized on the Lute," *JLSA* 7 (1974): 82-89.

1702 DUCKLES, Vincent. "Florid Embellishment in English Song," *AnnMl* 5 (1957): 329-45.

1703 GOMBOSI, Otto. "Stephen Foster and GregoryWalker," *MQ* 30 (1944): 133-46.

166

KOCZIRZ, Adolf. "Erwiderung auf O. Chilesotti," *ZIMG* 11   **1704**
(1909-1910): 235-36.

LAIBLE, F. "Lautenstimmung und Lautenbesaitung," *Die Gatarre*   **1705**
4/4-5 (1923).

MENDEL, Arthur. "Pitch in the 16th and Early 17th Centuries," *MQ*   **1706**
34 (1948): 28-45, 199-221, 336-57, 575-93.

MURPHY, Sylvia. "The Tuning of the Five-Course Guitar," *GSJ* 24   **1707**
(1970): 49-63.

NORDSTROM, Lyle. "Ornamentation of Flemish Chansons as Found   **1708**
in the Lute Duets of Francesco Spinacino," *JLSA* 2 (1969): 1-5.

POULTON, Diana. "Graces of Play in Renaissance Lute Music," *EM*   **1709**
3/2 (1975): 107-14.

PUTMAN, Aldrich. *The Principal 'agréments' of the Seventeenth and*   **1710**
Eighteenth Centuries: A Study in Music Ornamentation.
Unpublished Ph.D. diss., Harvard University, 1946.

SATOH, Toyohiko. "A Method for Stringing Lutes," *JLSA* 2   **1711**
(1969): 44-47.

SINGER, Gerhard. *Ludovico Zacconi's Treatment of the Suitability*   **1712**
and Classification of All Musical Instruments in the 'Prattica di
Musica' of 1592. Unpublished Ph.D., USC, 1968.

STRIZICH, Robert. "Ornamentation in Spanish Baroque Guitar   **1713**
Music," *JLSA* 5 (1972): 18-39.

VINCENTINO, Nicola. *L'Antica Musica Ridotta alla Moderna*   **1714**
Prattica, Rome 1555. Facs. ed. Kassel: Bärenreiter, 1959.

See also: **112.**

VIHUELA

BRENEN, Alfred. "Vihuela," *MGG* 13:1621-23.   **1715**

1716   DEVOTO, Daniel. "La música vocal de los Vihuelistas españoles," in *Dos Clases Públicas de historia de la Musica*. Mendoza: University Nacional de Cuyo, Cons. de Musica, 1945, pp. 39-81.

1717   ———. "Poésie et musique dans l'oeuvres des vihuelistas," *AnnMl* 4 (1956): 85-111.

1718   FOX, Charles W. "Accidentals in Vihuela Tablatures," *BAMS* 4 (1940): 22-24.

1719   GREBE, Maria E. "Modality in the Spanish Vihuela Music of the Sixteenth Century and its Influence in Latin-American Music," *AnM* 26 (1972): 29-59; 27 (1973): 109-29.

1720   MARTINEZ, Frank. "The Mystery of the Vihuela," *American Recorder* 15/1 (1974): 4-6.

1721   MYERS, Joan. "Vihuela Technique," *JLSA* 1 (1968): 15-18.

1722   POPE, Isabelle. "La vihuela y su música en el ambiente humanisticos," *Nueva Revista de Filologia Hispanica* 15 (1961): 365-76.

1723   PRYNNE, Michael. "A Surviving Vihuela de Mano," *GSJ* 16 (1963): 22-27.

1724   PUJOL, Emilio. "Les resources instrumentales et leur rôle dans la musique pour vihuela et pour guitare au XVIe siècle et au XVIIe," in *La musique instrumentale de la Renaissance*. Edited by J. Jacquot. Paris: CNRS, 1954, pp. 205-15.

1725   ROBERTS, John. "Some Notes on the Music of the Vihuelistas," *LSJ* 8 (1965): 24-31.

1726   SALAZAR, Adolfo. "El laud, la vihuela y la guitarra," in *Nuestra Musica*. Mexico, 1946, pp. 228-50.

1727   ———. *La Musica en Cervantes y otros ensayos*. Madrid, 1961.

1728   STEVENSON, Robert M. *Juan Bermudo*. The Hague: Nijhoff, 1960, pp. 15, 29, 42-49, 51-52, 56-57.

TONAZZI, Bruno. *Liuto, Vihuela, Chitarra e strumenti Similari*   **1729**
Nelle Loro Intavolatura, con Cenni Sulle Loro Letterature.
Ancona: Berben, 1971. 166p.

VOIGT, Alban. "Die Vihuela," *Deutsche Instrumentenbau Zeitung*   **1730**
38 (1937):58ff.

WARD, John. "Parody Technique in 16th-Century Instrumental   **1731**
Music," in *Commonwealth of Music.* Edited by G. Reese. New
York, 1964, pp. 208-28.

————. *The Vihuela de Mano and Its Music, 1536-1576.*   **1732**
Unpublished Ph.D. diss., New York University, 1953. 558p.
UM 71-28669.

ZAYAS, Rodrigo de. "The Music of the Vihuelistas and Its   **1733**
Interpretation," *GR* 38 (1973):10-11.

————. "The Vihuela: Swoose, Lute, or Guitar?" *GR* 38 (1973):2-5.   **1734**

————. "The Vihuelistas," *GR* 38 (1973):6-9.   **1735**

See also: 318, 337, 381, 481, 482, 484, 485, 486, 517, 575, 576, 578, 579, 669,
904, 953: pp. 18-82, 1112, 1121, 1137, 1518, 1675, 1690.

AUTHOR INDEX

171

addenda

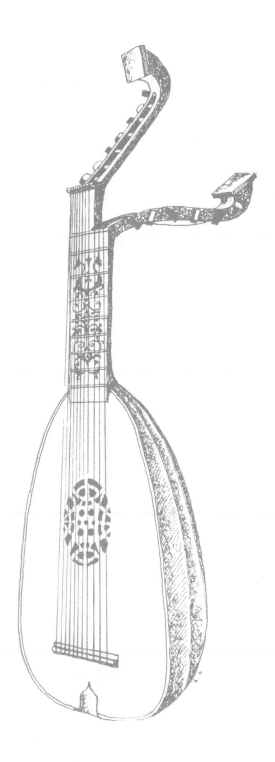

ADDENDA

The Addenda contains articles, editions and reviews examined from April 1976 through January, 1978. Abbreviations used in this Addenda are consistent with those used in the main work. In addition there are occasional cross-references to the citations in the main body–these will be obvious to the reader.

COMPOSERS / PERFORMERS–GENERAL BIOGRAPHY

GAUSSEN, Françoise. "Actes d'état-civil de musiciens français, 1651- **1**
1681," Recherches sur la musique française classique I (1960):
153-203.

JURGENS, Madeleine. Documents du Minutier Central Concernant **2**
L'Histoire de la Musique 1600-1650. Vol. II. Paris: La
Documentation Française, 1974.

CITTERN

GEISER, Brigitte. "Cister und Cistermacher in der Schweitz," **3**
Studia Instrumentorum Musicae Popularis. III. Festschrift to
Ernst Emsheimer on the Occasion of his 70th Birthday. January
15, 1974. Edited by Gustaf Hillerström. Musikhistoriska Museets
Skrifter 5. Stockholm: Nordiska Musikforlaget, 1974, pp. 51-56,
263-65.

WRIGHT, Laurence. "The Medieval Gittern and Cittole: A Case of **4**
Mistaken Identity," GJS XXX (May, 1977):8-42.

COMPOSERS / PERFORMERS—INDIVIDUAL BIOGRAPHY

ALEMANNO, Giovan Maria (Alemanus, Johannes Maria). *See:* 19, 24.

AMAT, Juan Carlos. *See also:* 111.

5   KING, A. H. "Amat's Guitarra Española," *EM* 4/3 (July, 1976):369. (Correspondence, reply to James Tyler.)

ATTAIGNANT, Pierre

6   CHIESA, Ruggero. "Storia della Litteratura del Liuto e della Chitarre. Il Cinquecento: Pierre Attaignant," *IFr* 4/15 (April, 1976).

7   ———. "Storia della Litteratura del Liuto e della Chitarra. Il Cinquecento: Pierre Attaignant," *IFr* 4/16 (July, 1976): 12-15; 4/17 (October, 1976): 14-17.

BAKFARK, Valentin

8   BENKÖ, Daniel. "Bakfark Problem I. (Lasso-Bakfark 'Veni in hortum meum')," *Studia Musicologica* XVII fasc. 1-4 (1975): 297-313.

9   MACHOLD, Robert. "Valentin Greff-Bakfark: 20 Jahre junger als bisher angenomen?" *Sudostdeutsche Vierteljahresblätter* XXVL/2 (1977): 81-86.

BATCHELAR, Daniel. *See:* 20.

BESARD, Jean-Baptiste

10   SUTTON, Julia. "The Music of J. B. Besard's Novus Partus, 1617," *JAMS* 19 (1966): 188-204.

BOESSET, Antoine. *See also:* 14.

11   MACHABEY, Armand. "Antoine Boesset (post Mortem)," *Recherches sur la musique française classique* II (1961-1962): 191-92.

BOSSINENSIS, Franciscus

CHIESA, Ruggero. "Storia della Liuto e della Chitarra. Il 12
Cinquecento: Joan Abrosio Dalza, Franciscus Bossinensis,"
IFr 2/6 (June, 1974): 14-20.

————. "Storia della Liuto e della Chitarra. Il Cinquecento: 13
Franciscus Bossinensis," *IFr* 2/8 (April, 1974): 26-32.

CAIGNET, Gabriel

MASSIP, Catherine. "Misique et musiciens à Saint-Germain-En- 14
Laye (1651-1683)," *Recherches sur la musique française
classique* XVI (1976): 117-52.

CAMPION, Thomas

LOWBURY, Edward, Timothy Salter and Alison Young. *Thomas* 15
Campion: Poet, Composer, Physician. London: Chatto &
Windus, 1970. 195p

CAPIROLA, Vincenzo

CHIESA, Ruggero. "Storia della Liuto e della Chitarra. Il 16
Cinquecento. Vincenzo Capirola. *IFr* 3/10 (June, 1975): 20-24.

CARA, Marco. *See:* 29.

CAVENDISH, Michael. *See:* 50.

CORBETTA, Francesco

PINNELL, Richard T. "Alternate Sources for the Printed Guitar 17
Music of Francesco Corbetta (1615-1681)," *JLSA* IX (1976):
62-86.

CORRETTE, Michel. *See:* 155.

CUTTING, Francis. *See:* 50.

DALLIS, Thomas

18   HARWOOD, Ian. "A Possible Dallis Reference?" *LSJ* XVIII
        (1976):46.

DALZA, Joan Ambrosio. *See also:* 12.

19   CHIESA, Ruggero. "Storia della Liuto e della Chitarra. Il
        Cinquecento. Giovan Alemanno, Joan Ambrosio Dalza," *IFr*
        1/4 (July, 1973):20-25.

DAY, Thomas

20   PHILIPPS, G. A. "Crown Musical Patrons from Elizabeth I to
        Charles I," *M&L* 58/1 (January, 1977): 29+.

DOWLAND, John. *See:* 149.

DOWLAND, Robert. *See:* 149.

DUBUISSON, Gabriel. *See:* 36.

DUBUT, ——. *See:* 139.

DUPRÉ, Laurent. *See:* 14.

FORD, Thomas. *See:* 20.

FRANCESCO da Milano

21   RADKE, Hans. "Zu R. Chiesas Ausgabe der Lautenkompositionen
        von Francesco da Milano," *Mf* XXVI/1 (January-March, 1973):
        77-81.

GAUTIER, Ennemond. *See:* 139.

GEMINIANI, Francesco

22   TONAZZI, Bruno. "Francesco Geminiani's 'The Art of Playing the
        Guitar or Citra'," *IFr* 1/1 (October, 1972):13-20.

GERLE, Hans

CHIESA, Ruggero. "Storia della Liuto e della Chitarra. Il   23
Cinquecento: Hans Gerle," *IFr* 5/18 (April, 1977):
24-28.

————. "Storia della Liuto e della Chitarra. Il   24
Cinquecento: Hans Gerle," *IFr* 5/19 (June, 1977):
15-18.

————. Storia della Liuto e della Chitarra. Il   25
Cinquecento: Hans Gerle," *IFr* 5/20 (July, 1977):
15-17.

————. "Storia della Liuto e della Chitarra. Il   26
Cinquecento: Hans Gerle," *IFr* 5/21 (October, 1977):
16-18.

GREAVES, Thomas. *See:* 50.

HÉDOUIN, Nicolas. *See:* 14.

HUREL, Charles. *See:* 36.

ITIER, Nicolas

DUFOURCQ, Norbert and Marcelle BENOIT. "Documents   27
du Minutier Central. Musiciens Françaises du XVIIIe
Siècle," *Recherches sur la musique française classique*
VIII (1968): 243-56.

JOHNSON, John

NORDSTROM, Lyle. "The Lute Duets of John Johnson,"   28
JLSA IX (1976): 30-42.

JUDENKÜNIG, Hans

CHIESA, Ruggero. "Storia della Liuto e della Chitarra. Il   29
Cinquecento: Hans Judenkünig, Bartolomeo Tromboncino,
Marco Cara," *IFr* 4/14 (June, 1976): 8-14.

30   HENNING, Rudolf. "Hans Judenkünig c 1455/60-1526: Commemorating the 450th Anniversary of His Death," *LSJ* XVIII (1976): 23-29.

LA BARRE, Pierre Chambanceau de. *See:* 14.

LAGNEAU, Pierre Henry. *See:* 27.

LE CAMUS, Sebastien. *See also:* 27.

31   BOULAY, Laurence. "Notes sur trois airs de Sebastien Le Camus," *Recherches sur la musique française classique* II (1961-1962): 54-60.

32   DUFOURCQ, Norbert. "Autour de Sebastien Le Camus," *Recherches sur la musique française classique* II (1961-1962): 41-52.

LE ROY, Adrian

33   HARWOOD, Ian. "On the Publication of Adrian Le Roy's Lute Instructions," *LSJ* XVIII (1976): 31-36.

LE SAGE DE RICHÉE, Philip Franz

34   REIMANN, Hugo. "Le Sage de Richée," *MfMg* XXI (1898): 10+.

MARCHAND, Jean-Baptiste. *See also:* 14, 35.

35   BENOIT, Marcelle. "Une dynastie de musiciens Versaillais: Les Marchand," *Recherches sur la musique française classique* I (1960): 99-129; II (1961-1962): 139-58.

MARCHAND, Luc. *See:* 35.

MARCHAND, Noel. *See:* 35.

MARTIN, Francois

36   ROBERT, Frederic. "La musique à travers le 'Mercure galant'," *Recherches sur la musique françasie classique* II (1961-1962): 178-79.

MATTEIS, Nicola

TILMOUTH, Michael. "Nicola Matteis," *MQ* XLVI/1 (January, 1960): 22-40.   37

MOLLIER, Louis de

BROSSARD, Yolande de. "Musique et bourgeoisie au dix-septieme siècle d'aprés les gazettes de Loret et de Robinet," *Recherches sur la musique française classique* I (1960): 46-49.   38

MAXFIELD-MILLER, Elizabeth. "Louis de Mollier, musicien et son homonyme Moliére," *Recherches sur la musique française classique* III (1963): 25-38. (English version in *Modern Language Notes* vol. 74 (1959): 612-21.)   39

MORLEY, Thomas

WELLS, Robin Headlam. "Thomas Morley's 'Fair in a Morn'," *LSJ* XVIII (1976): 37-42.   40

MOULINIE, Etienne. *See:* 150.

MUDARRA, Alphonso. *See:* 228.

NARVAEZ, Luis. *See:* 228.

NYERT, Pierre de

LE MOËL, Michel. "Chez l'illustre Certain," *Recherches sur la musique française classique* II (1961-1962): 71-79.   41

PHALESE, Pierre

KECSKES, Andras. "Fresh Data to 16th Century Hungarian Dance-Music (Almande de Ungrie)," *Studia Musicologica* XVII fasc. 1-4 (1975): 282-96.   42

PINEL, François. *See:* 14.

POURELL, Isreal. *See:* 139.

REBEL, Jean. *See:* 14.

RICHARD, François

43   Anon. "A travers l'inedit," *Recherches sur la musique française classique* II (1961-1962):230-33.

ROTTA, Antonio

44   FORIN, Elda Martellozzo. "Il Maestro di Liuto Antonio Rotta (d. 1549) e studenti dell' Universita di Padova Suoi Allievi," *Memore della Accademia Patavina* (Classe di Scienze Morale, Lettere ed Arti) LXXIX (1966-1967):425-43.

SCHLICK, Arnold. *See also:* 47.

45   CHIESA, Ruggero. "Storia della Liuto e della Chitarra. Il Cinquecento: Arnolt Schlick," *IFr* 2/9 (October, 1974):29-33.

STROBEL, Valentin. *See:* 139.

TROMBONCINO, Bartolomeo. *See:* 29.

VIRDUNG, Sebastian

46   CHIESA, Ruggero. "Storia della Liuto e della Chitarra. Il Cinquecento: Sebastian Virdung," *IFr* 2/8 (July, 1974):23-28.

47   LENNEBERG, Hans H. "The Critic Criticized: Sebastian Virdung and His Controversy with Arnold Schlick," *JAMS* X (1957).

DE VISÉE, Robert

48   DUFOURCQ, Norbert. *La musique a la cour de Louis XIV et de Louis XV d'aprés les memoires de Sourches et Lynes (1681-1758)*. Paris: Picard, 1968, pp. 21, 33.

DE VISÉE, (François?, Robert?)

49   MASSON, Chantal. "Journal du Marquis de Dangeau," *Recherches sur la musique française classique* II (1961-1962), pp. 200, 206.

WILBYE, John

PHILIPPS, G. A. "John Wilbye's Other Patrons: The Cavendishes 50
and Their Place in English Musical Life during the Renaissance,"
MR 38/2 (May, 1977):81-93.

WILSON, John

ARKWRIGHT. "John Wilson," *Grove* 5th ed. New York: 51
McMillan, pp. 311-13.

CONSTRUCTION

ABBOTT, Djilda and Ephraim SEGERMAN. "Gut Strings," *EM* 4/4 52
(October, 1976):430-31, 433, 435, 437.

DER MEER, John Henry van. "Musikinstrumentenbau in Bayern bis 53
1800," in *Musik in Bayern* vol. 2, ed. Robert Munster and Hans
Schmidt. Tutzing: Schneider, 1972, pp. 17-38.

DOWNING, John. "Lute Bridges and Frets," EM 4/3 (July, 1976): 54
365, 367. See *EM* (July, 1976) for reply by Djilda Abbott and
Ephraim Segerman.

FIRTH, Ian. "Acoustical Experiments on the Lute Belly," *GSJ* XXX 55
(May, 1977):56-63.

HELLWIG, Friedemann. "Zur Terminologie der europaischen 56
Zupfinstrumente. Das Vokabularium in der Quellen zum
historisches Lautenbau," in *Emsheimer Festschrift*, pp. 81-86.
(See no. 3 for complete title.)

LOWE, Michael. "The Historical Development of the Lute in the 17th 57
Century," *GSJ* XXIX (May, 1976):11-25.

SACCONI, Simone F. *I 'segretti' di Stradivari*. Cremona: Convegno, 58
1972, xvi. 261p.

TORTI, Francisco. "Materiali da costruzione del liuto: intervista 59
di Francisco Torti ad Andre Extermann, luitaio Svizzero," *IFr*
4/16 (July, 1976): 3-6.

EDITIONS

60 ADRIAENSEN, Emanuel. *Pratum musicum longe amoenissimum* . . .
Antwerp, 1584. Facsimile edition with an introduction by Kwee
Him Yong, University of Utrecht. Uitgiverij Frits Knuf B. V., Buren,
Netherlands, 1976.

61 ———. *Novum pratum musicum* . . . (*1592*). Facs. repr. Geneva:
Minkoff, 1977. 204p.

62 ALBERT DE RIPPE. Oeuvres d'Albert de Rippe, III: Chansons (deuzieme
partie); Danses. Edited by Jean-Michel Vaccaro. Paris: CNRS, 1975.

63 BACH, Johann Sebastian. *Johann Sebastian Bach: Drei
Lautenkompositionen in Zeitgenössischen Tabulatur.* Introduction
by Hans-Joachim Schulze. Leipzig: Zentralantiquariat der Deutscher
Demokratischen Republik, 1975, viii. 32p.

64 ———. *Fuga BWV 1000.* Critical edition and guitar transcription by
Alphonso Borghese. Milan: Edizioni Suvini Zerboni, 1975, xx. 11p.

65 ———. *The Prelude Fuga & Allegro* (*BWV 998*). Edited by David
Rhodes. Tablature, transcription and historical discussion. Boston:
Prelude Publications, 1976.

66 ———. *The Preludio con la Suite* (*Aufs Lautenwerk, BWV 996*). Edited
by David Rhodes, with tablature, guitar transcription and historical
discussion. Boston: Prelude Publications, 1976.

67 ———. *Johann Sebastian Bach for Solo-Lute.* Edited by Michael
Schäffer. Neuss/Rhein: Junghänel-Päffgen-Schäffer, 1976.

68 BAILLON, Pierre-Jean. *Nouvelle methode de guitare* . . . (*1781*). Facs.
repr. Geneva: Minkoff, 1977. 64p.

69 BAKFARK, Valentin. *Opera Omnia: The Lyons Lute-Book.* Edited by
Istvan Homolya and Daniel Benkö. Budapest: Editio Musica.

70 BELLIN, Julien. *Oeuvres de Julien Belin.* Introduction, transcription
and critical study by Michel Renault. Paris: CNRS, 1976.

71 BITTNER, Jacques. *Pièces de Luth* (1682). Facs. repr. Geneva: Minkoff,
1975. 120p.

BRICEÑO, Luis de. *Metodo mui facilissimo para aprender a tañer la*   **72**
guitarra a lo Español (1626). Geneva: Minkoff, 1972. 52p.

BYRD, William. *Lute Music of William Byrd*. Edited and transcribed   **73**
by Nigel North. London: Oxford University Press, 1976.

CAMPION, François. *Nouvelles decouvertes sur la guitarre contenantes*   **74**
plusieurs suittes de pièces sur huit maniéres differentes d'accorder
(1705) (=Paris, Bib. Nat. Vm7 6221). Geneva: Minkoff, 1977.
136p.

————. *Traité d'accompagnement et de composition (1716).*   **75**
Addition au traité d'accompagnement (1730). Geneva: Minkoff,
1977. 88p.

CARRÉ, Antoine, sieur de la Grange. *Livre de guitarre contenant*   **76**
plusieurs pieces . . . (1671). Geneva: Minkoff, 1977. 64p.

CUTTING, Francis. *Selected works for Lute*. Edited and transcribed   **77**
by Martin Long. London: Oxford University Press, 1971.

DELAIR, Denis. *Traité d'accompagnement pour le theorbe et le*   **78**
clavecin (1690). Geneva: Minkoff, 1972. 136p.

DOWLAND, John. *Lachrimae*. Leeds: Boethius Press (1976?).   **79**
Introduction by Robert Spencer.

————. *John Dowland: The Complete Lute Fantasias*. Edited and   **80**
transcribed by Stanley Buetens. Instrumenta Antiqua, 1975.

FLEURY, Nicolas. *Methode pour apprendre facilement à toucher le*   **81**
theorbe avec la basse continuee (1680). Geneva: Minkoff, 1972.
With Delair No. 78.

FRANCESCO DA MILANO. *Intavolatura de viola o vero lauto* . . .   **82**
Libro I, II (1536). Geneva: Minkoff, 1977. 136p.

————. *Francesco da Milano: Opere complete per liuto*. Edited   **83**
and transcribed by Ruggero Chiesa. Milano: Editizioni Suvini
Zerboni, 1972.

FRANCISQUE, Antoine. *Le Trésor D'Orphée* (1600). Geneva: **84**
Minkoff, 1973. 64p.

Editions

85 GALILEI, Michelangelo. *Il Primo Libro d'Intavolatura di Liuto* (1620).
    Transcribed by Ruggero Chiesa. Milan: Editzioni Suvini Zerboni.

86 GERLE, Hans. *Musica und Tablatur, auff die Instrument der kleinen und
    grossen Geygen, auch Lauten* (1546). Geneva: Minkoff, 1977. 216p.

87 ──────. *Tablatur auff die Lauten* (Nuremberg, 1535). Edited by Hélène
    Charnassé et Henri Ducasse. 4 vols. Paris: CNRS, 1976-1977.

88 ──────. *Tablature pour les luths* ... 1553. Transcription automatique
    par le Groupe E. R. A. T. T. O. du CNRS. Paris: (Publications de la
    Societé Français de Musicologie Ser. 5, vol. 1). Paris: Heugel, 1975,
    xvi. 85p.

89 GORZANIS, Giacomo. *Libro de Intabulatura di Liuto* (1567).
    Transcription and biographical study by Bruno Tonazzi. Transl. by
    Reginald Smith Brindle. Milano: Edizioni Suvini Zerboni, 1976.
    160p. (Musich Mus Ms 1511a).

90 GRENERIN, Henri. *Livre de guitarre* (1680). Geneva: Minkoff, 1977.
    104p.

91 GUERAU, Francesco. *Poema Harmonico* (Madrid, 1694). Facs. ed. with
    introduction and preface. London: Tecla editions, 1977. 88p.

92 LEIGHTON, William, Sir. *The Tears or Lamentations of a Sorrowful
    Soul.* Transcribed and edited by Cecil Hill. London: Stainer and
    Bell, 1970. (Early English Church Music, vol. 11.)

93 LOSY VON LOZINTAL, J. A. *Pièces de guitarre.* Edited by Jaroslav
    Pohanka. Musica Antiqua Bohemica, 38. Prague, 1958. (With
    tablature facs.)

94 MARCAS, J. J. R., ed. *Spain, Madrid, BN 6001.* Casa Editrice Editorial
    Alpuerto, S. A. 197-? Tablature and transcription.

95 MARCHERA, Fiorenza. *Canzona in G.* Edited by Howard M. Brown.
    Tablature and transcription. London: Oxford University Press,
    1975. 4, 16p.

96 MERCURE, (les). *Oeuvres de Mercure.* Transcribed and edited by J-M
    Vaccaro, Monica Rollin. Paris: CNRS, 1977.

MILLERAN, René. *Tablature de luth française.* (B.N. Paris, Res 823).   **97**
Introduction by François Lesure. Geneva: Minkoff, 1977. 256p.

NEWSIDLER, Hans. *Der ander theil des Lautenbuchs* (1536). Neuss/   **98**
Rhein: Junghänel-Päffgen-Schäffer, 1976.

PICCININI, Alessandro. *Intavolatura di liuto e di chitaronne, Libro*   **99**
primo (Bologna, 1623). Bologna: Antiquae Musicae Italicae
Monumenta Bononiensa, 1962.

PILKINGTON, Francis. *Complete Works for Lute.* Edited and   **100**
transcribed by Brian Jeffery. London: Oxford University Press,
1970.

PISADOR, Diego. *Libro de Musica de Vihuela* (1552). Geneva: **101**
Minkoff, 1973. 194p.

[Polish Dances]. *Tance Polskie.* Warsaw: Polskie Wydawnictwo   **102**
Muzycne, 1975.

RUIZ de RIBAYAZ, Lucas. *Luz y norte musical para camenar por*   **103**
las cifras de la guitarra español . . . (1677). Geneva: Minkoff,
1972. 172p.

ROOLEY, Anthony, ed. *The Compleat Beginner* (50 pieces selected   **104**
from Cambridge University Library Ms. Dd.2.11). Vol. 1.
London: Early Music Centre Publications, n. d.

————. *21 Renaissance Fantasies.* Vol. 2. London: Early Music   **105**
Centre Publications, n. d.

SIMPSON, Adrienne. *Music for the Lute.* London: Oxford University   **106**
Press, 1975.

de VISÉE, Robert. *Livre de guitarre* (1682); *Livre de pièces pour la*   **107**
guitarre (1686). Geneva: Minkoff, 1973. 158p.

————. *Suite in sol minore* (from *Livre de pièces pour la guitarre*   **108**
(1686). Edited by Alvaro Company and Vincenzo Saldarelli.
Milano: Edizioni Suvini Zerboni, 1975.

Guitar

109 WEISS, Sylvius Leopold. *34 Suiten für Laute Solo* (ca. 1720-1750) mit
Nachwort von Wolfgang Reich. Leipzig: Zentral Antiquariat der
DDR, 1976, xi. 280p. (Dresden Ms 2841-V-I.)

110 WEISS, Sylvius Leopold. *Music for the Lute: Original Tablature and
Modern Notation for the Keyboard.* Edited by R. Manahe. Tokyo:
Zen-On Music Co. Ltd., 1976.

GUITAR

111 HALL, Monica. "The 'Guitarra Española'," *EM* 4/2 (April, 1976).
(Correspondence, 227, 229. Reply by James Tyler on p. 229.)

112 POULTON, Diana. "Notes on the Guitarra, Laud and Vihuela," *LSJ*
XVIII (1976): 46-48.

113 STRIZICH, Robert. "Stringing the Baroque Guitar," *EM* 4/2 (April,
1976): 235, 237. (Correspondence; also reply by Donald Gill.)

See also: 22, 58, 331.

ICONOGRAPHY

114 BUCHNER, Alexander. "Musikinstrument auf der Freske der Karlsteiner
Apokalypse," [Musical instruments in the Fresco The Karlstein
Apocolypse] *Festschrift Emsheimer* I, pp. 32-41; II, pp. 259-61.
(See Cittern 3 for complete title.)

115 EDWARDS, David. "Dürer's Drawing 'Angel with a Lute'," *LSJ* XVIII
(1976): 43-44.

116 GODWIN, Joscelyn. "Main divers acors: Some Instrument Collections of
the Ars Nova Period," *EM* 5/2 (April, 1977): 148-59.

117 SAFFLE, Michael. "Lutes and Related Instruments in Eight Important
European and American Collections," *JLSA* IX (1976):
43-61.

INSTRUMENTATION

MONTEVERDI, Claudio. *L'Orfea: Favola in Musica*. Introduction   **118**
by Denis Stevens. Repr. of 1615 edition. Farnborough, G. B.:
Gregg, viii. 100p.

NEEMANN, Hans. "Die Laute als Generalbassinstrument,"   **119**
Zeitschrift für Hausmusik IV (1935): 39-45.

LUTE HISTORY / GENERAL

Anon. *"Lute Studies," Groupe D'Acoustique Musicale Bulletin*   **120**
No. 72 (February, 1973). Paris: University of Paris.

GRAME, T. "The Symbolism of the 'ud (lute)," *Asian Music*   **121**
3/1 (1972): 25-34.

HARWOOD, Ian. *A Brief History of the Lute*. London: Lute   **122**
Society Booklet 1, 1975?

See also: 112.

LUTE HISTORY / ENGLAND

COLLINS, David. "A Sixteenth-Century Manuscript in Wood. The   **123**
Eglantine Table at Harwick Hall," *EM* 4/3 (July, 1976): 275-79.

EMMISON, I. G. "John Petrie's Account-Books, 1567-1577," *GSJ*   **124**
XIV (March, 1961): 73-75.

KRUMMEL, D. W. *English Music Printing 1553-1700*. London: **125**
Oxford University Press for the Oxford Bibliographical
Society, 1976.

NORDSTROM, Lyle E. "The English Lute Duet and Consort   **126**
Lesson," *LSJ* XVIII (1976): 5-22.

127   OLDHAM, Guy F. "Import and Export on Musical Instruments in 1660," *GSJ* IX (1956):97-98.

128   SCHENK, Erich. "Englische Schauspielmusik in Österreichische Tablatur-Überlieferung," in *Sbornik Praci Filosoficke Faculty Brnenski University*. Brno: Philosophy Faculty, n. d., pp. 253-63. (Festschrift Jan Racek)

129   SCOTT, David. "Elizabeth I as Lutenist," *LSJ* XVIII (1976):45.

130   SEGERMAN, Ephraim and Djilda ABBOTT. "Stringed Instruments on the Eglantine Table," *EM* 4/4 (October, 1975):485. (correspondence)

LUTE HISTORY / FRANCE

131   BENOIT, Marcelle. *Musiques de Cour: Chapelle, Chambre, Ecurie, 1661-1733. Documents Recueilles.* Paris: Picard, 1971, xxii. 553p.

132   ————. *Versailles et les Musiciens du Roi 1661-1733. Etude Institutionelle et Sociale.* Paris: Picard, 1971.

133   BRENET, Michel. *Les Concerts en France sous L'Ancien Regime.* Paris, 1900. Repr. New York: Da Capo, 1970. 407p.

134   DUFOURCQ, Norbert and Marcelle BENOIT. "Les musiciens de Versailles à travers les minutes notoriales de Lamy versées aux archives départementales de Seine-et-Oise," *Recherches sur la musique française classique* III (1963):189-206.

135   LE MOËL, Michel. "Chez L'Illustre Certain," *Recherches sur la musique française classique* II (1961-1962):71-79.

LUTE HISTORY / GERMANY

136   TISCHLER, Hans. "The Earliest Lute Tablature," *JAMS* 27/1 (Spring, 1974):100-103, (Berlin Ms germ. qu 719 ca. 1470-1473.)

LUTE HISTORY / ITALY

CORTI, G. "Cinque Balli Toscani del Cinquecento," *RIM* XII/1   **137**
(1977): 72-82. (Florence B. N. Ms Magl. XIX, p. 31.)

PIROTTA, Nino. "Music and Cultural Tendencies in Fifteenth-   **138**
Century Italy," *JAMS* 19/2 (1966).

LUTE HISTORY / SCANDINAVIA

RUDEN, Jan Olav. "Stormakstidens 10 i Topp," *STMf* 58/2   **139**
(1976): 25-52

————. *Lut - och Gitarr-Tablaturer i Svenska Bibliotek och Samlingar.*   **139a**
Uppsala, 1967. Unpublished. (In numericode and polyphonic
transcription. No. 1120, B. S. Brook, Thematic Catalogues . . .)

LUTE INSTRUCTION / METHODS

SMITH, Douglas Alton and Peter DANNER. "How Beginners Should   **140**
Proceed. The Lute Instructions of Le Sage de Richee," *JLSA*
IX (1976): 87-94.

SOUTHARD, Marc. *Sixteenth-Century Lute Technique.* Unpublished   **141**
Master's thesis, University of Iowa, 1976.

WALLS, Kathryn. "John Dryden on Lute Playing," *EM* 4/4   **142**
(October, 1975): 491. (correspondence)

MANUSCRIPTS

AUSTRIA
Wien

KLIMA, Josef. *Die Lautenhandschrift von Schloss Schwanberg bei*   **143**
Deutsch-Landberg, St.: Bibliothek d. Ges. d Musikfreunde in Wien,
Sig. Mus. Ms 7763/92; Themeverzeichnis. Maria Enzersdorf bei
Wien: Verl. Wiener Lautenarchiv, J. Klima, 1975. 12p.

Manuscripts

CZECHOSLOVAKIA
Prague

144 KLIMA, Josef. *Die Lautenhandschrift des Joannes Aegidius Berner von Rettenwert (1603-1663) in der Musikabteilung des Nationalmuseums Prag, Sig. IV. G.18; Themenverzeichnis.* Maria Enzersdorf bei Wien: Verl. Wiener Lautenarchiv, J. Klima, 1975, vii. 61p.

ENGLAND
Oxford

Bodleian Library, Mus. School C94 "Gallot MS." See: **17**.

GERMANY
Munich

145 KLIMA, Josef. *Die Lautenhandschrift Munchen Mus. Ms 5362 der Bayerischen Staatsbibliothek: Themenverzeichnis.* Maria Enzersdorf bei Wien: Verl. Wiener Lautenarchiv, J. Klima, 1975, iii. 27p.

Gottweig

146 KLIMA, Josef. *Die Lautenhandschriften der Benedikterabtei Gottweig, N. O; Text, Tablatur 1, Anfangs d. 18 Jh., Tabulatur 2, 1735-1739; Thematische Verzeichnis.* Maria Enzersdorf bei Wien: Verl. Lautenarchiv, J. Klima, 1975. 59p.

ITALY
Florence

Florence Bib. Naz. Ms Magl. XIX, 31. See: **137**.

POLAND
Warsaw

Bib. Narodowa Muz. 366. See: **140**.

Wroclaw

Mf 2002; Mf 2003. See: **140**.

SPAIN
Madrid

MARCOS, Juan Jose Rey. "BN 6001," *Gendai Guitar* 8/3-4   **147**
(April-May, 1974). *See also:* **228.**

SWEDEN
Eriksbergarkivet

Eriksbergarkivet 52 c Gitarr-tablatur. See: **139.**

Kalmar

Kalmar Länsmuseum 21, 068. See: **139.**

Lund

Lund Univ. Bib. L34; Lund Univ. Bib. L37. See: **139.**

Stockholm

Katedralskolans Musiksamling 468 Gitarrtabulatur. See: **139.**

Musik Academi Tab. 3. See: **139.**

SWITZERLAND

SCHANZER, H.P. "Musik-Sammeldrucke des 16. und 17. Jahrhunderts   **148**
in schweizerischen Bibliotheken," *Fontes Artis Musicae* IV
(1957): 26, 38-42.

UNITED STATES
Washington, D. C.

WARD, John L. "The So-Called 'Dowland Lute-Book' in the Folger   **149**
Shakespeare Library," *JLSA* IX (1976): 5-29. (MS V. b. 280,
formerly MS 1610.1).

MUSICAL FORMS

ROMANCES. *See:* **230.**

SONG

150 BARON, John H. "Dutch Influence on the German Secular Solo-Continuo Lied in the Mid Seventeenth Century," *AMl* XLIII (1971): 50-51.

RELATED INSTRUMENTS

ARCHLUTE. *See:* **224, 225.**

BANDORA

151 ASHBEE, Andrew. "Brown (Braye) Bandora book—Instrumental Music from the Library of John Brown (1608-1691), Clerk of the Parliaments," *M&L* 58 (January, 1977): 43-59.

CHITARRONE

152 SPENCER, Robert. "The Chitarrone Francese," *EM* 4/2 (April, 1976): 164-66.

See also: **224, 225.**

MANDOLIN

153 COATES, Kevin. "The Mandoline an Unsung Serenader," *EM* 5/1 (January, 1977): 75, 77, 79, 81, 83, 85, 87.

154 ———. "The Neopolitan Mandoline," *EM* 5/3 (July, 1977): 427, 429. (Reply to Tyler, *EM* 5/2 (April, 1977).

155 LESURE, François. "La Methode de Mandoline de Michel Corrette (1772)," *Fontes Artis Musicae* 13 (1966): 72-76.

REVIEWS

167 ————. *Isagoge in Artem* . . . , ed. Schäffer, 1974.
  REV: P. C. *LSJ* XVIII (1976): 60-62.

168 BITTNER, Jacques. *Pièces de Lut* . . . (1682), repr. 1974. Junghänel-Päffgen-Schäffer.
  REV: Poulton, D. *EM* 4/3 (July, 1976): 331.

169 BREAM, Julien. *Dowland: Lute Works.* RCA ARL 1 1491.
  REV: Anon. *Gramophone* (January, 1977), p. 1161.

170 ————. *Lute Music of John Dowland.* RCA ARL 1 1491.
  REV: Anon. *Guitar Review* (January, 1977), p. 116.

171 *A Brief History of the Lute.* Harwood, Ian. London, 1975 [?].
  REV: Spencer, R. *EM* 4/3 (July, 1976): 313, 315.

172 CHANCY, ——. *Oeuvres de Chancy, Bouvier* . . . CNRS, 1967.
  REV: Dufourcq, N. *Recherches sur la musique française classique* VIII (1968): 66-67.

173 CUTTING, Francis. *Selected Works for Lute*, ed. M. Long.
  REV: Kirsch, D. *Mf* XXV/3 (July-September, 1972): 408-409.

174 DOWLAND, John. *Collected Works* . . . , ed. Poulton, D.
  REV: Chiesa, R. *IFr* 3/13 (October, 1975): 24-25.

175 ————. *Complete Lute Fantasias* . . . , ed. Buetens, S.
  REV: Kanazawa, M. *Notes* 33/4 (June, 1977): 939.

176 ————. *Lachrimae.* Leeds: Boethius Press.
  REV: Chiesa, R. *IFr* 5/20 (July, 1977): 31-32.

177 DUFAUT, ——. *Oeuvres de Dufaut*, ed. Souris, A. (*See:* **827**).
  REV: Tonazzi, B. *IFr* 3/11 (April, 1975): 31-33.

178 *Embellishing 16th-Century Music*, Brown, H. M. O. U. P., 1976.
  REV: Poulton, D. *LSJ* XVIII (1976): 62-66.

179 FRANCISQUE, Antoine. *Le Trésor D'Orphée.* Geneva: Minkoff.
  REV: Smith, D. A. *JLSA* IX (1976): 102-103.

180 FRESNO, Jorge. *Vihuelistas Españoles*, Hispavox HHS5, HHS10.
  REV: Chiesa, R. *IFr* 3/13 (October, 1975): 27-28.

Reviews

194 NEWSIDLER, Hans. *Ein Newgeordnet kunstlich* (1536), Junghänel-
 Päffgen-Schäffer, 1974.
 REV: Poulton, D. *EM* 4/3 (July, 1976):329.

195 *Notes sur l'Histoire de Luth en France*. Brenet, Michel. Turin, 1899.
 Repr. (*See:* 1187).
 REV: Smith, D. A. *JLSA* IX (1976):104.

196 PILKINGTON, Francis. *Complete Works for Lute*, ed. Jeffery, B.
 REV: Lendle, Wolfgang. *Mf* XXVI/4 (October-December, 1973):
 544-45.

197 RAGOSSNIG, Konrad. *Lute Music of the Renaissance: France*.
 Archiv 2533 304.
 REV: *Hi-Fi News* (May, 1976), p. 103.

198 ———. *Lute Music of the Renaissance: Germany and the Netherlands*.
 Archiv 2533 302.
 REV: *Hi-Fi News* (July, 1975), p. 91.

199 ———. *Music for the Lute: Italy*. Archiv 2533 173.
 REV: *Gramophone* (April, 1976), p. 840.

200 ———. *Musik für Laute: Italy*. Archiv 2533 173.
 REV: Chiesa, R. *IFr* 3/11 (April, 1975):34.

201 ———. *Music for the Lute: Spain*. Archiv 2533 183.
 REV: *Hi-Fi News* (July, 1976), p. 87.

202 ———. *Music for Two and Three Lutes*. Archiv 2533 323.
 REV: *Hi-Fi News* (December, 1977), p. 145.

203 ROOLEY, Anthony/Consort of Music. *First Book of Songe* (1597).
 DLSO 508-509.
 REV: *Gramophone* (November, 1976), p. 851.

204 ———. *Lachrimae* (1604). DLSO 517.
 REV: *Hi-Fi News* (October, 1976), p. 169.

205 SMITH, Hopkinson. *La Rhétorique des Dieux*. Das Alte Werk
 AW 6 42122.
 REV: Fallows, David. *Gramophone* (December, 1977), p. 1117.

Study of the Lute (1727). E.G. Baron, transl. D.A. Smith (*See:* **1199**).   **206**
    REV: Poulton, D. *EM* 5/2 (April, 1977):223, 225.

———.   **207**
    REV: Poulton, D. *JLSA* IX (1976):105-107.

Tance Polskie. Warsaw, 1975.   **208**
    REV: Chiesa, R. *IFr* (October, 1976), p. 28.

TYLER, James. *Music for Merchants and Monarchs*. Saga 5420.   **209**
    REV: Chiesa, R. *IFr* 5/20 (July, 1977).

———. *Music of the Renaissance Virtuosi*. Saga 5438.   **210**
    REV: Chiesa, R. *IFr* 5/20 (July, 1977).

TYLER, James, Anthony ROOLEY. *My Lute Awake!* L'Oiseau Lyre   **211**
    Sol 336.
    REV: Chiesa, R. *IFr* 3/12 (1975):37-38.

VAUMESNIL, Sr. de. *Oeuvres de Vaumesnil, Edinthon* . . . CNRS, 1974.   **212**
    REV: Dufourcq, N. *Recherches sur la musique française classique*
    16 (1976):198-99.

VISÉE, Robert de. *Suite in Sol minore*, ed. Company, A.   **213**
    REV: Anon. *M&L* 58/1 (January, 1977):117-18.

WEISS, S.L. *Music for the Lute*, ed. Manache, R.   **214**
    REV: Brown, H.M. *EM* 5/3 (July, 1977):413.

TABLATURE / TRANSCRIPTION

Anon. "Opinioni dei Partecipanti al convegno di Chicago sui problemi   **215**
    della transcrizione moderna," *IFr* 2/9 (October, 1974):8-18.

BOETTICHER, Wolfgang. "Die alteren Lautentabulaturen und das   **216**
    Problem ihrer Klassifizierung," *KONGRESS 1970*, pp. 345-49.

DANNER, Peter. "D'adattamento della musica barocca per chitarra   **217**
    all'esecuzione moderna," *IFr* 2/8 (April, 1974):11-20.

218 LONARDI, Masimo. "Del sonare il basso overo la realizzazione liutistica dell basso continuo," *IFr* 5/21 (October, 1977): 7-15.

219 MEYLAN, Raymond. "Limites de l'objectivite dans les écritures instrumentalse de la Renaissance," *Informatique Musicale* (October, 1973), pp. 1-9.

220 SOURIS, André. "Apport du repertoire du luth a l'étude des problémes d'interpretation," in *L'Interpretation de la Musique Française aux XVI éme et XVIII éme Siècle*. Paris: CNRS, 1974. Pp. 107-20.

THEORBO

221 SPENCER, Robert. "Chitarrone, Theorbo and Archlute," *EM* 4/4 (October, 1975): 406-23.

222 WRIGHT, Laurence. "Theorbo, Archlute and Chitarrone," *EM* 4/4 (October, 1975): 497. (correcpondence)

TUNING / ORNAMENTS

223 BROWN, H. M. "Accidentals and Ornamentation in Sixteenth-Century Intabulations of Josquin Motets," *Proceedings of the International Josquin Conference* (forthcoming).

224 ————. *Embellishing Sixteenth-Century Music*. Oxford University Press, 1976.

225 ————. "Embellishment in Sixteenth-Century Italian Intabulations," *PRMA* 100 (1973-1974): 49-84.

VIHUELA

226 BARON, John H. "Secular Spanish Solo Song in Non-Spanish Sources, 1599-1640," *JAMS* XXX/1 (Spring, 1977): 20-42.

HALL, Monica. "The Vihuela Repertoire," *EM* 5/1 (January, 1977):   **227**
     59, 61, 63, 65. (Review article on various recordings).

MARCOS, Juan Jose Rey. "Ramillete de Flores Inedite per Vihuela,"   **228**
     IFr 4/15 (April, 1976): 15-23.

POULTON, Diana. "A Vihuela in Ecuador," *LSJ* XVIII (1976):   **229**
     45-46.

SIMPSON, Glenda and Barry MASON. "The Sixteenth-Century   **230**
     Spanish Romance. A Survey of the Spanish Ballad as Found
     in the Music of the Vihuelistas," *EM* 5/1 (January, 1977): 51,
     53, 55, 57.

WYTOSZYNSKYI, Leo. "Vihuela und Gitarre im Spiegel neuer   **231**
     Literatur," *ÖeMZ* 30 (April, 1975): 186-93.

See also: 112.

AUTHOR INDEX

213